Making Love Real

Making Love Real

The Intelligent Couple's Guide to
Lasting Intimacy and Passion

Danielle Harel PhD & Celeste Hirschman MA

Making Love Real
By Danielle Harel PhD and Celeste Hirschman MA

Published by Somatica Press
Cover Design: Yair Harel

This book is not intended as a substitute for the medical advice of physicians. The reader should regularly consult a physician in matters relating to his/her health and particularly with respect to any symptoms that may require diagnosis or medical attention.

Printed in the United States of America

ISBN 10: 0692525483
ISBN 13: 9780692525487

First Edition

Somatica Press

ACKNOWLEDGEMENTS

Creating loving relationships is what makes the world go round and we could not have written this book without the loving help and support of our family, friends, colleagues, clients and students. We'd like to thank our families, Yair Harel and Dimitry Yakoushkin, for supporting us and helping with every aspect of this book and a special thank you to our children Sitar Harel, Shiraz Harel and Devin Yakoushkin for teaching us how to listen and for teaching us what love is really all about. Thank you to our editor, Hilary Roberts, who smoothed out the rough edges. A big thank you to Magick, Dr. Megan Ducheck, Courtland Allen, and Jon Hull for reading earlier drafts and offering essential suggestions and edits. And thank you to those of you who helped us sort through our name brainstorm: Allegra Hirschman, April Hirschman, H. R. Bremner, Keeley Rankin, Dalia Perez and Elena Letourneau.

MAKING LOVE REAL

K eenan and Sarah came to see us after having been together for
a little over 12 years. "It's not that we are unhappy, exactly,"
Sarah told us. "Things just seem off." When we asked them about
the relationship's beginning, Keenan, with a gleam in his eye, said,
"At first Sarah wouldn't give me the time of day. She thought I was
going to be flaky and a player. But when I saw Sarah for the first
time, I thought, 'This is the most gorgeous woman I've ever met
and I'm going to do whatever it takes to get her.'"

Sarah started laughing. "I thought he was super sexy too, but
he was so light and easy about everything, I was sure he just wanted
to play around. Here we are, 12 years and two kids later."

When we asked them how they are now, they looked at each
other helplessly, and Keenan finally tried to explain. "Everything
seems to upset Sarah. I do the same things I've been doing for
years, play in my band, go out with my friends, but she gets so upset, and then I feel like I can't do anything right. I wish she could
just accept me for who I am."

Sarah continued, "It's not like I want him to give up his
friends. I just wish he was more focused on us, on me and the

family, and when I ask for that he eventually gets pissed off and defends himself, and finally shuts down completely. Needless to say, we rarely have sex these days, we can't seem to communicate about anything, and we're both so busy we can't get ahead of the curve."

Keenan nodded and finished, "Yeah, she's just angry a lot of the time. I really thought I could make Sarah happy, or I wouldn't have chased after her so hard."

You Want to Have a Real and Loving Relationship

If you have picked up this book, we assume that, like Keenan and Sarah, you want to have a long-term, fulfilling, and loving relationship where both of you can be accepted for who you really are. Keenan and Sarah's story is a very common one. They met, fell in love, and, with the tools they had, forged a beautiful relationship. Over time, they began to notice that the qualities they had once found so sexy and adorable, like Sarah's almost OCD-like organization and Keenan's absent-minded spontaneity, began to get on each other's nerves. They had little spats and wavered between trying to change each other and trying to return to their earlier happiness.

Like Keenan and Sarah's, all relationships have challenges. There can be many barriers that get in the way of love and fulfillment, and being in a relationship is rarely simple or easy. While our society has the fantasy that relationships last a lifetime, most relationships do not last forever and more than half of all marriages end in divorce. Whether or not you end up being together forever, a relationship is an opportunity to go deeper into who you are, to grow, and to feel loved and connected. Research shows that the best predictor of individual happiness is being surrounded by a loving family, friends, and community.

During the highs, relationships offer love, deep connection, excitement, nurturing, acceptance, joy, sharing, and companionship. During the lows, they bring pain, fear, insecurity, conflict, and disappointment. What most people don't realize is that ups and downs in relationships are completely normal.

The experience of seeing others have relationships or having them yourself teaches you a lot about what it is like to share your life with another person. Unfortunately, the relationship examples in our society rarely offer a road map for consciously creating the supportive and satisfying relationships you'd like to have. As sex and relationship therapists, we have studied, experimented with, and explored the different relationship road maps. We have worked with countless couples to help them create the relationships they truly desire. Through our work we have developed the Somatica Method – a road map to sustainable sex and intimacy that will help you and your partner Make Love Real by meeting your incredible potential for love, connection, and pleasure in your relationship.

The Problem with Current Road Maps to Relationship Success

The current road maps that are available to teach you about relationships generally take one of two approaches – attachment or individuation – and then offer couples ways to improve their relationships based on one of these models.

Proponents of the attachment approach remind you that you need the bonds of **love** to survive as a species. This is true: human survival is predicated on the ability to form long-term attachments with caregivers. As you move from the parent-child relationship into adulthood and romantic love, your basic need for attachment persists. In a relationship, if your sense of attachment is threatened, you go into survival-like fight, flight, or freeze patterns, which often lead to relationship-damaging behaviors. In the attachment model, the focus of therapy is to maintain the relationship by helping each person in the couple understand the other's fears and anxieties and shift their own behaviors to minimize these fears and strengthen the attachment. This is what Sarah is focused on, and it is one of the two key relationship needs.

Proponents of the individuation approach point out that, in order to have a fulfilling life and relationship, you must be **real** in a relationship. In other words, you have to be true to your authentic self and follow your deepest desires without letting your partner's fears and anxieties stand in the way of this self-actualization. In this model, the way to a fulfilling relationship is for each of the individuals to be true to themselves and to work on their own fears and anxieties so as to support their partner in being real as well. This is what Keenan is focused on, and it is the other of the two key relationship needs.

Both of these methods have merits, but each fulfills only half of what you need from a relationship. As Keenan and Sarah are discovering, a combination of love and being real is necessary to a fulfilling relationship. Striking the delicate and ongoing balance of creating safe attachment and being true to yourself in a relationship is the focus of the Somatica Method and what you will learn in this book.

Let's look at one of Keenan and Sarah's fights through the lenses of attachment and individuation. Every time Keenan goes out for a ride on his motorcycle, Sarah is afraid he is going to die. While Keenan is away, images of him crashing and dying spin through her head. She sees herself alone and destitute with their two young children. She feels shaky and fearful and is so worked up that, as soon as Keenan walks in the door, she starts yelling at him about how selfish he is to put her through this all the time. Keenan feels like his wife doesn't care at all about his need for freedom to be himself. Sarah then gets defensive and shuts down, spending time in her art studio until she thinks Keenan has calmed down and it is okay to come back out.

An attachment road map would help Keenan see that Sarah isn't just being crazy, that she is actually having a fight, flight, or freeze response. While her way of sharing with Keenan is not helpful, she is trying to tell him that she loves him, depends on him, and fears for his life, her life, and the lives of their children. If only Keenan could see that his wife is terrified and not just judging and attacking him, he would stop riding the motorcycle in order to help her feel safe and stable.

While a sense of attachment is essential to long-term relationship success, and is foundational to people's sense of safety and connection, the problem with the attachment road map is that couples often over-compromise. In other words, they give up on their individual needs for the sake of the relationship, which often leads to resentment, midlife crisis, and emotional disconnection or ending the relationship because the it demands that they not be their true selves.

The individuation road map, on the other hand, is based on the idea that you do not always have to be enslaved to childlike fears. It is about helping couples to grow up, move beyond that scared child inside, and accept their partner's need to be who they are. They are focused on freedom, self-actualization, and the understanding that you cannot and should not control others.

In the case of Sarah and Keenan, an individuation road map would help Sarah grow up and face her fears. Sarah would be encouraged to have compassion and sympathy for Keenan's desires, take an actuated, adult perspective on how he expresses his self-hood, and develop a grown-up sense of safety within herself. A therapist using this model would point out that Keenan is not riding his motorcycle to hurt Sarah but that his motorcycle riding is an essential part of his sense of self. The therapist would help Sarah see that she cannot control everything and that if Keenan stops riding his motorcycle he might lose his sense of self and freedom in the relationship, causing resentment and distance. Instead of stopping Keenan's riding, Sarah could support his desire to ride and thus support him in being true to himself.

Individuation is also essential to relationships and important to people's long-term fulfillment, growth, and acceptance of who they are. The problem with the individuation road map is that people are expected to just "grow up" and "get over" their fears of loss, abandonment, and insecurity all on their own. Unfortunately, your wounds and insecurities are not so easily overcome – you cannot just will them away; you need to heal them, and you can only do this by being vulnerable with the people you love. The feeling that you need to get over your fears creates a sense of shame when you cannot. To avoid feeling this shame, people do not let themselves be vulnerable, so their relationships stay distant and superficial. In order to deepen your relationship, you must be able to share your strengths as well as your fears and insecurities.

The Somatica Method: A Holistic Road Map for Making Love Real

What we have found in working with countless couples is that every human being needs *both* a sense of attachment and a feeling that they are free to be who they are. This is the only way to have a sustainable relationship—to Make Love Real. The truth is that good attachment creates safety and trust, allowing people to explore who they are and move towards self-actualization. At the same time, when your partner supports you in being true to who you are, you feel more accepted and therefore more attached.

At the beginning of a relationship, people naturally tend towards creating attachment. As they feel more attached and safe, they begin to want to fulfill their own personal dreams and desires, and this is where conflict starts to arise. Through the Somatica Method, we help each individual in a couple learn how to identify their own individual needs, while at the same time helping them learn how to understand their own and their partner's fears and care for each other in the midst of these fears. The Somatica Method focuses on interdependence and supports both attachment and freedom.

This, of course, is much more easily said than done, and it takes real work and commitment to create this kind of relationship – but it is the most sustainable relationship you can have. If you want a lifetime of deep connection, fulfillment, and pleasure, you need to

cultivate attachment, make space for survival fears, and build empathy and resilience. With these tools you can support your partner in being true to who they are.

In our work with Keenan and Sarah, we helped Keenan see the
ways his actions brought up Sarah's attachment fears. We also helped
Sarah see that Keenan's desire to ride was about his identity and was
not a personal attack on her. After each of them was able to empathize with the other's needs—the need for attachment and the need
for individual freedom—Sarah felt ready to support Keenan in riding and Keenan felt comfortable making changes to his riding habits.
He agreed that he would not ride on rainy days and that he would
only ride at night once a month. They both agreed that they would
listen to each other – Keenan to Sarah's fears and Sarah to Keenan's
need to be true to himself. This is an example of how the Somatica
Method supports both attachment and individuation needs and invites couples to bridge and connect through their differences.

Disappointment: What the Other Road Maps Leave Out

Long-term relationships provide you with an opportunity to grow
because they cause you to face your deepest longings and fears
as you connect with another human being whose needs, feelings,
and desires differ from yours. Similarities between you and your
partner and attunement to differing needs help you relax into a
sense of safety and stability. This relaxation creates a foundation
for growth. At the same time, the challenging differences between
you and your partner provide the growth-promoting tension in
your relationship. In the face of these differences, we have found,

some amount of disappointment is not only inevitable but also an important path to growth and a deeper connection.

While there are no studies measuring the fulfillment you get from a relationship, we would guess that a really good relationship gives you about 70% of what you want. This means that you will experience at least 30% disappointment. While most people don't want to think about disappointment, we have found that couples who have an empowered approach to disappointment have the most successful and resilient relationships. We do so much work with couples on dealing with disappointment in their relationships that we felt disappointment deserved its own section in this book.

After all, almost every relationship problem derives from the inherent differences between any two people and the misunderstandings and disappointments that come from those differences. These may be differences that seem trivial, such as disagreement about how clean the house should be, or differences that most people would see as highly challenging, such as disagreement about practicing non-monogamy versus monogamy. The Somatica Method reflects our belief that learning how to navigate your differences and the disappointments that come from them is an essential part of relationship success. In this book you will learn tools to deal with disappointment in order to move from stagnation and isolation into expansion and cohesion.

What's Sex Got to Do with It?

Sex can be a big part of the glue that holds people together in relationship. When you have sex, hormones that promote bonding and relaxation are released and help to keep you connected and lower the day-to-day frustrations that couples face. Sex is a way that you can express your love and desire for your partner as well as experience acceptance for your uniqueness, therefore sex can be an expression of both attachment and individuation. Unfortunately, the attachment and individuation road maps both fall short when it comes to creating a healthy and satisfying sex life.

The attachment approach assumes that if you have good attachment and communication, warm, loving, and fulfilling sex will follow. The individuation road map suggests that if each of you just pursues what you want sexually from your partner, you are most likely to get it. Both of these approaches can be helpful to create a great sex life, but they are not enough. Sexual knowledge and skills don't develop merely as a result of being more connected or pursuing your sense of self. Since we have so little good education and information about sex, in order to have a great sex life, you will also need to learn about sex, what makes it hot as well as the sexual skills involved in achieving this hotness.

Because our society trivializes sex and shames us for our sexual desires, modern-day couples generally have limited understanding of sex and many end up in low-sex or sexless relationships. They know very little about their options, and therefore experience the bare minimum sexually. They think that sex is just about positions, orgasms, and the new hot tip of the week. But sex is so much more than that. It is about a desire to be met and accepted, sexually as well as emotionally. This is why the Somatica Method doesn't assume sex will just happen. We help our clients overcome negative socialization around sex and fill in the learning gaps that this socialization has created.

We have found that, for sex to be great, couples need both a solid connection and the ability to know what each person wants, and they need to find ways to support each other in pursuing it. Because no two people are alike and no two people are interested in exactly the same thing, people need to be able to communicate what they want and need. Unfortunately, socialization around sexuality is very negative and that makes it very difficult for people to know what they need, let alone honestly and openly communicate about it. In the section on sex, we will introduce you to a large sexual and emotional menu, as well as help you identify what you like on that menu. On this journey you will develop a language of sex, arousal, and desire. You will learn to let go of the idea that sex should just happen and approach sex as something you are cultivating on an ongoing basis. By doing this, you can create the sexual connection that is right and fulfilling for you and your partner.

How to Use This Book

This book is full of in-depth information and practical exercises that will help you and your partner become more connected, empathetic, loving, and turned on by each other. Not every part of this book will be helpful for every couple who reads it. We invite you to find the chapters and exercises that feel most inspiring and important to you. When you follow your desire and delight and when you feel ready for something more than just going through the motions, it is much more likely to result in transformation and satisfaction.

You don't have to believe every single word written in this book or complete every single exercise to get something out of it. Just taking the time to read, share, play, and practice with your partner around your relationship will either help bring you closer together or bring whatever challenges you are having to the surface.

If you find that those challenges are arising and you need more help than just this book, you can reach out to us and our practitioners for help. Sometimes when habits and patterns have formed over long periods of time and there is built-up resentment, it can be very difficult to get out of the negative patterns on your own. Also, sometimes it's just fun and exciting to have another person help you expand and try out new experiences that you might not even know are possible. Either way, we are here to help.

PART 1

CULTIVATING INTIMACY

C ouples who have the most successful relationships know that cultivating intimacy means doing both tension and connection well. Moments of connection, such as touching, looking at one another, having an enjoyable shared experience, talking or having sex are all part of the glue that keeps relationships together. Likewise, moments of tension including differing desires, disagreements, misunderstandings, hurt feelings and anger, if done well, can also be part of the glue that holds your relationship together. When you come to conflict with the intention of sharing difficult feelings and deepening empathy and understanding of one another, and you learn to repair breaks in connection, you begin to build a sense of trust for one another that you can make it through challenges. Since every relationship has tension, knowing that you can make it through challenging moments is also part of the glue that holds relationships together. Doing both connection and tension well are both essential to sustainable love.

What Is Love?

It feels so good to say and to hear the words "I love you," but what do they really mean? In order to talk about what makes a relationship successful, it is important to have a working definition of love and understand why we choose the people we choose to love. Most relationships start out with a feeling of attraction and then move into two somewhat distinct phases. The first is the experience of falling in love (the "honeymoon period"), and the second is the experience of long-term loving.

Attraction: Why You Choose Your Partner

While it is true that part of attraction may be physical, much of it has a lot more to do with familiarity (and often physical attraction is also based on a particular kind of familiarity). It is no coincidence that the root word of "familiarity" is "family": when you choose a partner, if you feel very attracted to and excited about them, it is likely because they remind you of someone who had a strong effect on you as a child. This attraction may come from a desire for an opportunity to resolve some of the hurts that you experienced as a child, and/or to re-experience some of your positive childhood moments.

If one of your parents was distant, you might choose someone who is distant as a way to attempt to fulfill your child's desire to finally succeed in drawing a distant person closer. Or, if you had a parent who was very dramatic and intrusive, you might choose someone who has familiar behaviors in an attempt to have a different, rewarding experience where your boundaries are respected by someone with a similar personality.

Unfortunately, many relationships are simply a replay of these old negative patterns. Your inner child's desire for repair is real, but when confronted with the familiar behaviors of your chosen partner, your inner child's protective strategies take over. Instead of growing, you find that your habits take over: you become clingy with a distant partner or coldly push an intrusive partner away. While you are attracted to what is familiar in your partner, unfortunately, that person also responds to you in the painful, familiar ways, and you both fall into what we call a "negative relationship vortex" with limited tools for repair. The negative relationship vortex is the way that your and your partner's wounds and protective strategies interact and we will go deeply into the vortex and how to repair it later in the book. We've found that if you and your partner are willing to learn self-awareness and change old habits, you can find more satisfying and sustainable ways of relating that you may never have experienced as a child. These new ways of relating will offer you the joy, fulfillment, and longevity that you have been trying to create in your relationships.

Taking the Fall

Researchers, therapists, and the media generally refer to the first six to eighteen months of any relationship as the "honeymoon period." In the beginning, you don't know what will happen between the two of you and you don't know much about the person with whom you are trying to connect. You look at this other person and imagine that they are everything you desire. In this phase, you and your partner are generally on your best behavior, marketing yourselves with everything you've got, downplaying your challenges and basking in the delight of someone seeing you as amazing and perfect.

Your uncertainty about this person's desire for you creates a constant longing for connection, which often takes the form of sexual desire. You may feel infatuated and have obsessive thoughts, as well as an inability to concentrate on your day-to-day life. In addition, your sex hormones are spiking in attempt to bond you together long enough for baby-making, so sex is generally spontaneous, passionate, and full of uninhibited desire and arousal. You are probably filled with feelings of excitement as you imagine all of the possibilities for your future together.

Many people are so addicted to this phase that as soon as a relationship starts moving towards the stability and deeper certainty of long-term love, they move on to their next one. They start a new honeymoon period, never making room for their partner's flaws or getting comfortable with accepting and revealing their own. If you make it through the honeymoon period, you have a chance at long-term love.

Long-Term Love

As you move through the honeymoon period, you start to see the person for who they really are, which is never exactly the person you hoped or imagined they would be. This is the beauty and challenge of a relationship – the differences between your fantasy partner and the person sitting in front of you create an opportunity for interpersonal and personal growth.

In the long-term love phase, you get to see your partner's endearing and annoying day-to-day habits, as well as your own, and you also get to experience your partner's and your own vulnerability and defenses. As you let someone in more deeply and they let you in, you begin to see and feel your strengths and challenges. Each of you starts to gain access to the other's buttons that trigger the fears of the inner child, the fight/flight/flee response that comes in the face of these fears, as well as the accompanying defensive strategies.

We believe true and lasting love is about developing a solid, loving base supporting each other's attachment needs and giving each other mutual care. It is also about personal growth, following your own dreams and desires, and celebrating and supporting your partner in growing and actualizing their dreams and desires as well.

All Relationships Have Conflict

The fantasy of the perfect relationship creates an unattainable image of eternal happiness. In this fantasy, you are completely in tune with your partner, you fulfill all of each other's needs and desires without ever having to be asked, and you never hurt each other. While the desire for attunement and pleasure is beautiful, the expectation that your partner will be able to fully meet those needs may be the single most damaging belief standing in the way of sustainable relationships.

The fantasy of eternal happiness creates an atmosphere of constant disappointment where you keep comparing yourself and your partner to unattainable ideals and imagining that everyone but you has reached them. You feel like a failure any time you fall short of the fantasy. The fantasy says that your true match, or soul mate, should be the fulfillment of all of your longings. When they are not, you feel that they are purposely trying to hurt you by not meeting your needs. You walk around feeling like you've failed and you assume everyone else has the blissful happiness that is unattainable for you.

Holding on to this dream keeps you from receiving the tremendous benefits that relationships actually have to offer. Two people who come into a relationship have different needs, desires, histories, outlooks, habits, cultures, families, and social expectations about how people are supposed to behave. Because of this, misunderstandings and conflict are unavoidable. If you believe that a good relationship means that you will always be happy and without conflict, you will never feel content and satisfied with your relationship. Relationships can fulfill some of your most important human needs, including intimacy, acceptance, support, connection, pleasure, and understanding. At the same time, they inevitably bring challenges, hurt, pain, and fear. Being in a loving relationship allows you to deepen intimacy, give each other pleasure, and feel loved through moments of joy, celebration, and excitement and, amazingly, also in moments of grief, conflict, and tension.

In addition to having the unfulfillable fantasy of eternal happiness, most people are also given a poor model for responding to differences and tensions. As a society, we look at tensions in relationships as problems that need to be resolved, overcome, and never repeated. You are not told that tension offers amazing opportunities for growth and deeper intimacy. You learn that conflict is to be avoided or resolved quickly, with the underlying premise that all problems in relationships are resolvable.

In the best examples given by society and popular culture, conflict is resolved when the guilty party is identified, they apologize, and the injured party forgives them. In the worst examples, there is blaming, shaming, betrayal, and explosions. Yet neither of these approaches leads to understanding, intimacy, and growth.

To experience the amazing growth and repair that moments of tension offer, you must have an understanding of your wounds and compassion for the ways that you protect yourself in the face of these wounds. You cannot get rid of the impulse to employ defensive strategies that so effectively protected you in the past, but you can accept them with compassion and learn to do something different when they arise.

In order to do something different you need a host of new tools. With these new tools, you and your partner have the opportunity to experience a much deeper and less conditional love for yourselves and each other than you may have ever had in your lives before. You learn that you can feel fulfilled and connected even when there are problems that are not resolvable. You also learn that empathy, acceptance, and support are much more powerful tools of love and intimacy than blame and shame, or even apology and forgiveness.

In this book you will learn about your and your partner's inner children, what it means when they surface, and how to approach them. You will learn not to take it all so personally, so you can get on the same team. You will learn how to vote for connection instead of protection and to identify (and therefore be more intentional about) your actions in the face of your triggers. You will learn to lead with vulnerability, to understand and share your needs and capacities, and to respect your own and your partner's boundaries. You will learn how to effectively communicate and to solidify your attachment to each other while honoring your individual needs.

Meet Your Inner Child

In order to do tension well, you need to have an idea of where the roots of much of the tension in relationship begin. So much of what we learn about love, intimacy, and relationship happens during our childhoods. During your childhood and adolescence, you related to your parents, siblings, extended family, friends, and community, and you had times of connection and times of loneliness. You had wonderful, enhancing experiences in your childhood where your sense of self was supported and accepted, but no one has a perfect childhood. There were times when your parents or the adults who were supposed to support and protect you failed or when you faced challenges and difficulties that you didn't have the support or capacity to fully process. Because your childhood was integral to the person you've become, in times of challenge or tension your inner child can show up with its hopes and its defenses. We find it very helpful to look at this inner child as both hurt and hopeful. The inner child protects against the wounds of the past and dreams of a different future where your true self can be seen and accepted.

It is helpful to picture your inner child as a young person inside of you that gets activated when you are treated in a way that reminds you of how you were treated poorly as a child. When this happens, in a desperate attempt not to be treated that yucky way again, your inner child takes over by making life decisions for you. This child uses the best defenses and strategies it had at the time it was wounded and also makes attempts to help you be seen for who you really are. Sadly, these tools are often ineffective and destructive to intimacy because they are the tools of a child and not an adult. Anne and Jack offer a perfect example of the way your childhood shapes your relationship challenges.

After her birth, Anne's mother suffered intense postpartum depression. Her mother would cry every time she tried to nurse Anne, and she eventually ceded most of the parenting responsibilities to her husband and a part-time nanny. In Anne's adult life, she married Jack, who suffers from cyclical depression. Whenever he goes into a depression, she dissociates, losing her ability to stay in her own body or to listen to or talk with Jack about his feelings. As a newborn baby, you have very few tools, and leaving the body when things are too difficult is one of the few options you have. Unfortunately, Anne's dissociation leaves Jack feeling even more desperate and alone.

When Jack was three, his father left his mother for another woman. Jack felt sad and alone but saw how much pain his mother was in and worked hard to attend to her in hopes that she would cheer up and provide for his needs. When many of those needs went unmet, he learned to rely on himself. Now whenever Jack feels sad, instead of reaching out he turns inward and tries to take care of everything on his own. This leads to his relying solely on himself, pushing others away, and eventually falling into depression. When Anne dissociates in response to his depression, it confirms his beliefs that he negatively impacts others and that he has to take care of himself, which makes him even less likely to reach out.

The way Anne's and Jack's wounds are interacting with each other creates a negative relationship vortex. A negative relationship vortex is when your response to your deepest hurts (for example, Anne's dissociation) activates your partner's deepest hurts (Jack's belief that no one can help him) and their response (Jack's self-isolation) activates your deepest hurts (Anne's abandonment). This interaction of hurts and responses to those hurts creates a self-perpetuating negative cycle that leaves both partners feeling lonely and disconnected. However, a beautiful opportunity exists in the midst of the Relationship Vortex, an opportunity to turn the vortex into a positive cycle of healing.

Know Your Inner Child's Fears

Part of getting out of the vortex is understanding that this young, hurt inner child is always scanning for the threats that originally hurt it. If you look back into your childhood and see what your parents were able to give you and what they were not, what your experiences with other adults and children were like and what kinds of challenges you faced, you can see the threat or threats for which your inner child may be scanning. This doesn't mean you have to think your parents were terrible or blame them (after all, they didn't have perfect childhoods either); it is simply a way to better understand your fears and your habitual reactions to threats. Recent research shows that even great moms are only about thirty percent successful in attending to their babies' needs, meaning we all have plenty of needs that go unfulfilled, even in the most ideal of childhoods.

In the case of Jack and Anne, Jack sees Anne's depression as another indication that his needs won't be met, and he is also afraid of being too much of a burden on her. He is always scanning for ways that he can avoid causing those he loves further pain and distress. Ironically, he tries to do this by keeping his sadness away from Anne, leaving her feeling alone and abandoned. Anne is scanning for the threat of abandonment, which in her case took the form of her mother distancing from her as a result of depression. Whenever she sees a depressed or detached face, she feels like she is going to lose the relationship, just as she lost her early relationship with her mom. Her automatic response to a depressed face is to dissociate. When Jack sees Anne dissociate, he feels even more like a burden. This is how Jack and Anne perpetuate their negative relationship vortex.

Depending on what happened to you when you were young, you might be scanning for many different kinds of threats. You will see these threats everywhere, even when they are not really there or are of a much smaller scale than you fear. When you see a threat, you get triggered, meaning you have an immediate emotional re-action. For example, when your partner is late coming home and doesn't call you, you feel that you are not important to them and you feel hurt or angry. In reality, they care deeply about you but were stuck in an important meeting. These are some common threats that you might scan for:

Nobody will love me.
No one cares about what I need.
Someone will physically or emotionally hurt me.
No one will think I'm worth investing in.
No one really wants to know me.
No one wants to care for me.
No one would accept me if they truly knew me.
No one will love me unless I do everything right.

At the end of this chapter you will find an exercise to help you identify your own and your partner's threats.

Care for Your Inner Child

Now you know that you and your partner each have an inner child who is scanning for some kind of threat, and you have begun to identify your negative relationship vortex. Now what? The first step in turning the vortex around is to develop a relationship with your inner child. Developing a positive relationship with your inner child means learning to treat yourself gently and give yourself the love, connection, and support that you need.

First you must identify your "go-to" defensive reactions – the automatic reactions and habits you developed in response to perceived threats. Common go-to reactions include dissociation, shutting down, lashing out, doing it all yourself and not involving your partner, letting your boundaries be crossed, asserting your will over others, trying to get constant attention, and putting up with whatever comes your way even if you don't like it. You developed these strategies as a child in order to survive the emotional (and sometimes physical) threats you faced in childhood. Most people feel very judgmental about their own and their partner's defensive reactions and just want them to disappear.

It is important to know that these defensive responses probably won't go away. Your inner child's habitual defenses will generally be your "first responders," like firefighters who arrive first at a disaster scene. Once you become familiar with your most common defensive responses, you can begin to see them arise. This is called developing a "witness" or gaining self-awareness of your defenses. As soon as the defensive responses surface, see if you can have compassion for that little child, who is fighting like hell, running away, or shutting down in order to survive. This is the time to thank your inner child for using those defenses to help you survive. Once you thank it and be kind to it, having compassion for the little child and why it needed those responses in the first place, it will feel attended to and seen, and you can then choose to try a different response.

As Jack and Anne began to see their patterns in the relationship, they were able to catch the first signs of their habits instead of fully diving into them. When something happened in Jack's life that made him feel sad, he could start to see the ways he would talk himself out of sharing those feelings with Anne, telling himself that she didn't need any more pain. He was surprised to find out that Anne was very comfortable with his external expression of sadness and that expressing these feelings actually kept him out of the numbness of depression. He found that Anne dissociated only when he didn't express sadness and felt more connected to him when he shared his feelings, regardless of whether they were positive or negative. Jack's opportunity to change his habitual response was to share thoughts and experiences that made him sad early and often. Overall, this meant less depression and more connection with Anne, and it also meant that Anne's dissociation was triggered much less often.

For Anne it was helpful to recognize that, while Jack did get depressed, he always came back, and he wasn't leaving her alone in the way that her inner child had been left alone in the past. When she would see Jack's depressed face, she would visualize holding her little child and saying, "Don't worry, he's just a little out of it sometimes, but he always comes back." Anne also began to recognize the early signs of dissociation and to gain some tools to help bring her back into her body. She noticed that when Jack would make "the face," her first feeling was that she was beginning to float out of her body. She found that touching and tapping her face, arms, and legs at this point helped her get back into her body. She also realized that the pounding of her feet against the pavement during her early-morning run literally jogged her back into her body. When she noticed herself dissociating, she could also reach out to

Jack, share her experience. She might say, "Hey, Jack, I'm feeling floaty", and ask him for touch. Notice that Anne needed elements from both the individuation model of relationships (taking care of herself as an adult and reminding herself, "He'll be back") and the attachment model (reaching out for touch).

One way to think about your relationship with your inner child is to think of your adult self as the caregiver and advocate for your inner child out in the world. If your inner child needs some help or soothing, you can help it. You can also ask your partner or other supportive people in your life for help. In addition to learning about and caring for your own inner child, you can learn to empathize and help care for your partner's inner child. This is how the Somatica Method differs from other road maps – it offers a comprehensive set of tools to promote both individuation (self-care) and attachment (care for and support of your partner).

Understand Your Partner's Fears

Now that you have learned more about your own defenses, you can begin to have empathy and compassion for your partner's inner child, the threats for which it is scanning, and its defenses. When people look at their partner's reaction to something, they often trivialize it, as our client Andrew did in talking about his wife, Soo-jin: "It was such a little thing and she got so upset about it. It didn't make any sense. I feel like I'm being made out to be the bad guy when all I did was forget to turn the heater off before I left the house. Sure, it ran for three days while we were away, but what's the big deal? Then we get home and she looks at me with this utter disappointment in her eyes and starts lecturing about how much it costs, which I'm guessing was about seven dollars."

The problem with this logic is that it is looking at the surface event, which may indeed be quite trivial, without seeing the underlying hurt or trigger that the event has touched. As soon as you see what the event is triggering, you will see that the reaction is very much aligned with the level of hurt and fear that your partner is experiencing. If we take the brief example above of the heater being left on and look at it in relation to Soo-jin's childhood, we can see what was going on for her under the surface.

Soo-jin's parents were together until the day they died, but Soo-jin always wished they had separated. Soo-jin described her father as a "big shot with no money to back it up." While her parents both worked at the family business, her father controlled most of the money and was always outspending the company profits. Her father loved to entertain prospective customers and show off for his friends. He would treat customers to extravagant dinners and go out drinking, stay out all night, and come home with very little to contribute to the household. He spent their revenue on everything from expensive cigars and scotch to the new, updated car he felt he needed to buy. At one point their debt got so high they almost had to sell the business, and the entire family feared losing all that they had built.

As the oldest of four siblings and the only girl, Soo-jin was the first to become aware of the suffering and stress her father's spending caused her mother. Her mother didn't even consider divorce an option. At fourteen Soo-jin got a job to help contribute to the household and ease her mother's pain. She felt like she was the only responsible one in the house. Andrew, on the other hand, came from a financially comfortable, middle-class family whose culture was to approach life with a laid-back attitude. While he liked the structure and beauty Soo-jin brought into his life and their home, he also felt that she was "pretty uptight."

Soo-jin shared with us how she felt when she saw that the heater had been on all weekend: "I just flipped. It felt so unfair. I felt like if I didn't keep track of everything it was all just going to slip away again. It also made me think of all the times Andrew bought himself the little extra things he wanted and the way I never do that for myself. I love Andrew's easygoing approach to life – it's part of why I married him – but sometimes it just takes me back to the feeling that I am the only financially responsible person in the house, and I lose it. I know it doesn't make sense, but him calling me crazy or overreacting does not help."

As Andrew saw Soo-jin's pain and tears, he realized that his leaving the heater on was just a symbol of her father's behavior and was neither trivial nor about him. He began to understand that Soo-jin was scanning for being responsible for everything and for wastefulness. He started to put himself in her shoes and better understand her inner child's pain. "God, Soo-jin, that sucks," he said. "I can't even begin to imagine the pressure you were under, and you were just a kid. When I was fourteen the thing I was most worried about was whether I was going to get that new skateboard I wanted."

By understanding and empathizing with your partner instead of trivializing, dismissing, or defending yourself, you can find the emotional logic that drives their seemingly irrational response. Once your partner feels your understanding and empathy for their experience, they feel not only powerful relief and connection in the moment but also the reparation of many years of carrying that pain all by themselves. This is one of the many reasons relationships can be so healing. In addition, you get to feel like someone your partner can really depend on and with whom they can share themselves vulnerably and fully. When you help your partner, you feel elated, confident, and good about yourself.

Share the Responsibilities of Inner-Child Care

As a team, you can learn to take care of your own and each other's inner children. If you see your partner's inner child come out and start using some of its old defenses, you can offer a different experience from the one they had as a child. You can give them, in the present, the kind of care they needed back then. You can also ask for the kind of inner-child care you need.

Anne and Jack provide a useful example of how partners can learn to take the initiative in caring for each other's inner children. In addition to Anne's learning to notice when she was dissociating and using her own tools to combat it, Jack learned to identify that "out of body" look in her eye. When he saw it, he could check with her to see if she needed help. If he came close to her in that moment, looked directly at her, and said firmly, "Anne, look in my eyes, baby. I'm right here. I'm not going anywhere," it would often help Anne return to her body even more quickly than when she practiced her touching and tapping. Jack found that, even if he felt depressed, it was very fulfilling to help Anne get back into her body. It counteracted the idea that he was always causing pain and gave him an opportunity to soothe Anne's pain instead. It often helped him immediately feel less depressed.

If Anne saw that Jack was starting to go into a depressive state, she would ask him to tell her everything that was hard or painful for him, even if it was about her. During these times Anne learned not to take anything Jack said as permanent, because it was all being seen through the dark glasses of his depression. They had an agreement that she would just listen without feeling like she had to change herself or fix any of Jack's problems. She was relieved to have something more empowered to do than dissociate, and Jack got the experience of not feeling all alone in his pain.

Through the story of Jack and Anne we hope you noticed that helping your partner's inner child not only feels good for your partner but also often has great rewards for you. It is very powerful to be able to soothe the person you love when they are hurting. Just as Anne learned to ask Jack for help when she was feeling floaty, you too can learn to move beyond your defensive reactions and offer opportunities for your partner to soothe you. In the case of Jack and Anne, their defensive reactions created fears in their partner, but they were not overtly attacking. We will talk later in the chapter about how to deal with more aggressive or hurtful defensive responses.

Challenges to Inner-Child Care

While engaging with your and your partner's inner children, you may run into some challenges. You may look into your history and not have any clue about the origin of your triggers. You may hate the responses of your own or your partner's inner child, or you both might get triggered at the same time. You may also experience an imbalance where one person feels like they are always responsible for taking care of the other when they are not receiving any care.

Not knowing the origin of your triggers. If you are having a strong reaction to something that your partner is doing, a reaction that feels out of proportion, then you are triggered. But what if, when you search in your memories, no matter how deep you look, you can't find a clear connection between this experience and past experiences? Don't doubt your reaction. Some painful experiences happen before you have the ability to remember them or the words to describe them. Trust your body and trust that this sensitivity came from somewhere; otherwise you wouldn't be having this re-action. Treat yourself with compassion and honor this area of sensitivity regardless of whether or not you know its origins.

Hating the inner child. You might experience a strong reaction to your own inner child or your partner's. You might feel angry towards these parts and that they are pathetic or useless. Because you experienced moments of powerlessness, terror, shame, or humiliation as a child, it is understandable that your gut reaction might be to distance yourself from this hurt part. It is important that you notice these feelings, since they will help guide you into relationship with this child and see the way that it suffered. The more you try to get rid of these insecure, fearful parts, the more they will insist that you pay attention to them. Avoiding them will require you to shut down parts of yourself and miss out on many of the amazing gifts vulnerability and intimacy have to offer.

All the adults have left the building. Often when one of you is triggered and reacting, the other will get triggered too and react back. This is a moment when "all of the adults have left the building" and there are two triggered children duking it out. These are the most difficult moments in any relationship. In these moments the best thing to do is acknowledge that all the adults have left. You might try taking a time-out where both of you stop trying to figure it out. You can sit quietly, take a break from each other, or distract yourselves with something so that at least one and hopefully both of you can come back to using all of the new tools you will find in this book. If one of you is triggered by the thought of abandonment, you can sit quietly together or agree on a short time span you will be apart.

Imbalance in inner-child care. It is very important that both people in a relationship learn how to care for their own and their partner's inner child. Sometimes relationships end up with a large imbalance, where one person ends up caring for the other's inner child much of the time without receiving any care themselves.

In the long term this kind of imbalance can be very damaging because it sets up a parent-child dynamic in the relationship. This kind of imbalance causes burnout and lack of sexual desire – after all, you don't want to feel like you are having sex with a child; you want to have sex with an adult, an equal partner who can nurture and be nurtured. If one of you is feeling resentful about being the one who always has to give care, it is important for the resentful partner to bring up this imbalance. Sometimes you may need help from others, including folks who can take over some of the care like your family or friends or a therapist who can help you gain balance.

The following exercise will help you start to make some connection and acquire self-awareness about your own inner child and gain insight and empathy for your partner's.

Exercise: Inner Child Visualization

The Inner Child Visualization is a way to reconnect with the inner child inside you who felt hurt and left behind in some way. See if you can follow the feelings and sensations inside your body more than thinking your way through the visualization. Also, one note of caution: you will be journeying back to a childhood memory. If you have had severe trauma (such as physical or sexual abuse) in your life and have not yet processed it, we suggest that you do not go back to one of these memories on the first time around with your inner child. Start with something that is not too intense so you are not triggered into a trauma response.

Even though creating a relationship with your inner child is an individual journey, you can do it as a couple. You will want to sit or lie down near each other and close your eyes. Begin to take some slow, deep breaths and allow your chest to expand. Feel the breath moving towards your stomach, feel your stomach rise and fall, and then allow the breath to move all the way down towards your pelvic floor.

As you breathe deeply, let yourself float back through your memories, as if turning the pages of the album of your life. Let yourself float back in time to the earliest memory you have where you felt sad, hurt, excluded, punished, disappointed, etc. If you don't know what memory to choose, just let your mind settle on one. You can always go back and visit other memories, and every memory is an opportunity to connect with your inner child.

Once you have landed in one of these early memories, take some time to inhabit the memory. Try to bring in all of your senses so that you can really immerse yourself in the memory. Notice where you are and who is there with you. Notice your surroundings, sights, sounds, smells, what you were wearing, and other details of the experience. Notice your emotions in the experience (sadness, confusion, anger, etc.) as well as the bodily sensations that go along with those emotions (tightness in your stomach, fire in your chest, numbness all over your body). You can even let your body respond to the memory. For example, if you feel your shoulders begin to tighten and curl inward, allow your shoulders, maybe even your whole body, to curl up into a tight ball.

Once you are fully immersed in the experience, bring your adult self to your inner child and love it! See what your inner child needs from you in that moment. It may need some kind of physical comfort, like being picked up and held, being hugged, or having its hair stroked. It may need to hear some comforting words of understanding, such as "I know you felt left out when Mom and Dad fought, and that was really hard, but I will never leave your needs and feelings out." Whatever your inner child needs the most, give that to it. If any feelings of anger, rejection, or harshness towards your inner child arise, see if you can step back and find some compassion for yourself and the little child inside you. You may have had a lot of criticism in your life. See if you can offer something different in this moment, like acceptance and empathy.

Once you have made a strong connection with your inner child, let it know that you are there with it now and will be happy to listen to its feelings anytime, support it, soothe it, and advocate for it out in the world from now on. Give your inner child the message that it doesn't have to be alone anymore, and invite it to tell you whenever it needs some love or care. After you have taken plenty of time to love your inner child, slowly and gently return to the present moment and feel your inner child there with you now. Think of this as an ongoing, lifelong relationship where you make the commitment to continue to listen and stay connected with your inner child. In this way you can provide your inner child with what it needed but didn't get early on.

Journal opportunity: Your Inner Child
If you like to journal, it can be great to journal on your relationship with your inner child.

Share Your Visualizations
To feel closer and more compassionate about each other's hurts and defenses, it is very helpful to take a moment to share with your partner where you went on this visualization journey and what you learned. Tell your partner about your childhood experience and how you soothed your inner child. Be specific about the words or gestures that you used that felt the best. Demonstrate to your partner what kind of touch or holding your inner child liked and have them do it back to you.

1. Identify and share the threats for which you are scanning. Common threats that people scan for are being unimportant or nothing, abandonment, criticism, being left out, being unlovable, being misunderstood, being punished or humiliated, and feeling powerless.

2. Share with your partner a few ways that you commonly defend yourself from these threats. Common defenses include shutting down, lashing out, distancing, dissociating, leaving before you get left, and collapsing.

3. Now that you know more about your inner child, as well as its threats and defenses, brainstorm some ways that you and your partner can start caring for your inner child when these threats arise. In the upcoming chapters we will talk about many ways to care for your own and your partner's inner child. For now, see if you can come up with some inner-child care ideas together.

Understand Your Habitual Responses

Couples who have the most success in creating lasting, loving, and fulfilling relationships are those who understand their habitual responses and continue to vote for connection over protection. When you are fearful that you are going to be hurt again in the same way your inner child was hurt, your limbic system activates. This is a part of your brain that monitors for your emotional and social well-being, and it responds with an automatic fight, flight, or freeze response in the face of a physical or emotional threat. It tells you to protect yourself at all costs. When you act in this fight, flight, or freeze mode, the cost is often a loss of intimacy.

Because people are social animals and can survive only as a group, everyone has a built-in fear of abandonment and social ostracization. These fears and the limbic activation that follows them are felt most acutely in people's closest relationships. Thus, most people will experience fight, flight, or freeze when their partner threatens to leave them or when they feel shame in the face of their partner's real or perceived disapproval.

People also experience fight, flight, and freeze responses around less threatening situations, especially when they have had additional reinforcement of these threats during the course of their lives. For example, if you were abandoned, pushed away, or ignored by one or both of your parents as a child, you may experience some level of fight, flight, or freeze response to situations to which other people do not. If you had an experience of abandonment, you might feel intense fear when your partner turns away from you in anger or is packing to leave for a trip. If you were shamed, criticized, left out, or physically punished or abused as a child, you may feel a fight, flight, or freeze response when your partner says something mildly critical of you or, evening teasingly, calls you a name. You have fight, flight, or freeze responses in the face of moments of tension and conflict with your partner because they represent all those fears of being alone and ostracized.

When you are emotionally threatened, your neocortex – your thinking brain – is blocked and your limbic system, which is not capable of complex thought, takes over. You feel an overwhelming urge to take the fastest route to relief of the panic and terror, even if that route is destructive to your relationship. In this state, you feel intense internal pressure to fight or get away from the threatening stimulus (in this case, your partner). In intimate relationships, the fight response often takes the form of spilling out all of your angry, negative thoughts about your partner or wanting to hit or hurt them in some way. The flight response often takes the form of locking yourself in a room, taking an angry "break," hanging up the phone, giving the silent treatment, or driving away. The freeze response might be an inability to move, think, or talk. When you are dealing with your partner in fight, flight, or freeze, there is no way to reason with them. We will talk more about this in the section on listening.

You have already started to be aware of the wounds of your inner child and to give your partner the benefit of the doubt that they want to be on your team. Next you can slowly but surely learn to move beyond your habitual self-protective responses. In order to do this, you will first need to map those responses to triggers to see where you may be able to interrupt them and do something different.

Exercise: Map Your Triggers

As you learned above, when you are triggered, your limbic system takes over, you go into auto-response mode, and then you often take some kind of protective action. This usually happens so quickly that you have neither awareness of nor choice in any of these responses or actions. It can be helpful to "study" your protection mode from a relatively calm place, so that you can tell the difference between your relaxed and triggered states. In order to develop this awareness, you can start by purposefully experimenting with triggers.

Take a few moments to come up with a sentence that your partner has said or might say that has triggered you or that you know would trigger you. Sit with your partner and have them say the sentence to you. Some example sentences are "I'm going to take a break and be by myself for a while," "You always think of yourself first," and "I am attracted to your friend Alex." Choose the sentence yourself; do not have your partner pick it for you! When your partner says the sentence, don't take any immediate action. Instead, take a moment to notice three things:

1. What do you feel in your body? For example, do you feel tightness, heat, shutting down, floating, tension? Where do you feel it in your body? For example, you might feel it in your head, face, stomach, chest, or all over.
2. What kinds of thoughts are rushing through your head? "I knew it. They don't give a shit about me." "Here we go again." "I just can't do this anymore." "Fine, I guess this is just how life is. Might as well learn to put up with it." "I wish they would stop torturing me and just go away."
3. What kinds of things do you want to do or say in order to protect yourself? For example, you might feel like stomping out and slamming the door, hitting someone or something, yelling at the other person about how insensitive and horrible they are, or curling up in a ball and crying, or you might lose your ability to speak or think.

The partner who just spoke the sentence should notice what they see in their partner's face and body. This way, they will be better able to recognize when their partner is triggered. Make sure you both get a turn in each role. Take some time to share what happens to you in these triggered moments.

Having a deeper awareness of your automatic reactions will help you recognize when you are triggered. It is important to note that sometimes a triggered child looks very much like a "reasonable" adult. For example, some people become very calm and logical when they are triggered and explain coolly why what the other person is doing is unreasonable and how they should proceed. Culturally we think of this as the "right" response, yet this logical, intellectualized approach is as much a triggered child's strategic defense as screaming or slamming the door is. It is still a disconnected, detached, and protective stance.

Get on the Same Team

At the beginning of a relationship you feel like you are building a team with your new love. The experience of falling in love with your partner feels like diving into a warm pool of affection, safety, excitement, and joy. You often feel like you have found someone who understands you and is on your side. You feel like the two of you together can face the ups and downs of the outside world. You trust that your sweetheart wants the best for you. As you begin to spend time together and start tripping over each other's triggers, you can lose the sense that you are on the same team and start to see the other person as someone causing your pain and problems. This shift is an indication of how much you are attaching to them.

Oddly enough, it is a good sign – it means you trust them enough to let them into your vulnerable parts. When you trust someone, you unconsciously feel safe to do your emotional work with them as your deepest hopes, fears, expectations, and insecurities arise. You long for your partner to be perfectly attuned to all of your needs and to care for you lovingly when you feel hurt. This wish resembles the the build in longing that children have for their parents to be perfectly attuned to their every need before they even had the words to ask. This child part wants your partner to know exactly what you need and how to soothe you without your ever have to teach them how.

This fantasy persists in our cultural image of the perfect soul mate, who knows us deeply and automatically because they are our "other half." It sets you up for endless disappointment as you continue wishing for this attunement and silently building resentment as your partner fails over and over again. You begin to question whether or not they are your soul mate and instead imagine that they are wrong for you or, worse, that they are purposely trying to hurt you.

Sadly, we do not grow up seeing examples of people honestly sharing their needs and gently and lovingly teaching their partners how to care for them when they are in pain. Instead, we see the adults around us blaming, shaming, shutting down, etc. and using all of their defenses in futile attempts to save themselves from disappointment.

In our work with couples, we have found that it is quite rare that people purposely try to hurt each other. In general, they are trying to stay true to themselves or attempting to make their partner happy, albeit in all the wrong ways. When one person in a couple is actually purposely trying to hurt the other, that is an indication of how hurt and backed into a corner that person feels. It is also an indication that they do not have the tools to do anything else – such as ask for what they need, share a vulnerable hurt, or set a boundary. Instead of assuming your partner is trying to hurt or torture you, hold onto the idea that they actually really want to be on your team – as long as it doesn't mean giving up who they are. By assuming that they want to be on your team, you are giving them the benefit of the doubt, believing that although they are do-ing their best, neither of you has taken the time to share vulnerably, empathize, and ask for what you want in a non-blaming way.

Carlos and Jonathan are a perfect example of a couple who wanted desperately to be on the same team but were going about it in all the wrong ways.

The first two years of Carlos and Jonathan's relationship was like a dream. In the love-'em-and-leave-'em town of San Francisco, they had both resigned themselves to a fun life of casual sex and long-term friendships, yet each had dreamed of having a long-term love that he could count on. When they met, they both figured it would be somewhere between a one- and five-night stand and then they'd be out on the prowl again, but they couldn't get enough of each other. And soon they both started to realize it was more than just sex. They spent most of their time together, took each other into account in all of their decision making, and actively supported each other's dreams and goals.

About a year and a half into their relationship, things started to spiral out of control. Throughout their courtship, Carlos had been on partial disability and working only part time. Jonathan had never experienced anything like the kind of attention and af-fection he got from Carlos. Carlos was romantic and attentive in ways Jonathan couldn't have even imagined possible. To Jonathan, it literally felt like Carlos could read his mind. Carlos cooked his favorite foods and was waiting at home for him every day when he got home from work. Carlos was always planning some new, fun adventure for them out in the world or a quiet, romantic night at home with the latest art film, and he seemed to have an endless appetite for sex.

However, three months before they came to see us, Carlos had gotten a new job at a startup company and begun working ten-hour days. He would arrive home later than Jonathan, he never had time to go out, and most nights he was too exhausted to even think about sex. Jonathan was devastated. He felt that Carlos must have fallen out of love with him. He began to get short and angry with Carlos all the time, belittling him and criticizing his new job.

When asked, Jonathan talked about how happy his childhood had been. His mother, he said, was extremely warm, affectionate, and supportive of him. When, at fourteen, he came out to her as gay, she threw him a coming-out party where the two of them celebrated and she insisted he tell her all about the boys he had crushes on.

When asked about his father, Jonathan described their relationship quite differently. "My father just had the title of 'father,' but he never really even knew what that meant. Honestly, I'm not sure I know what a father is supposed to be like. He was always calm, never emotional, and he spent most of his time out of the house. He didn't even have the excuse of being a workaholic; he just found ways to never be home."

Jonathan's father would go to the local bar and watch sports as many nights as possible. On the weekends he always had new home-improvement projects that required shopping and planning and executing. When he wasn't doing home improvement, he would lock himself in his office and build model airplanes. Underneath his desire to separate from the family and do these projects was a critical attitude towards Jonathan and the family in general. Young Jonathan astutely picked up on this critical attitude, and he learned two things. First, wanting his dad's approval, Jonathan's strategy was to emulate his dad and try to be "good." Second, he adopted a critical voice towards himself and others, taking on his dad's buried but ever-present criticism.

Jonathan told us, "I did everything I could to get his attention: played the sports he liked, learned how to build model airplanes, and helped with the home-improvement projects when I didn't have homework or practice, but no matter what I did, I could tell that at best he was indifferent. Honestly, I think I chose Carlos because he was nothing like my dad. He is literally the most passionate, emotional person I have ever met. But apparently he no longer feels that way about me."

Carlos, on the other hand, was brought up by a single mom. Overworked and exhausted most of the time, his mother generally spoke to Carlos only to remind him what he should be doing or tell him what he was doing wrong. She was very critical of herself, feeling she had wasted her life, and she took those feelings out on Carlos. Carlos told us, "It was like she was Dr. Jekyll and Mrs. Hyde. Most of the time, she would nit-pick everything I did – how I looked, what I wore, who my friends were – then, every once in a while, it felt like I was supposed to be her partner or something. She would start to cry and tell me how she wasted her life, she would tell me that she was a terrible mother and apologize for being so mean to me, and then she would want me to hug and cuddle her until she calmed down. I felt like she only saw me when she needed something. The rest of the time, I was just her whipping boy."

If we look at Jonathan's story, we can see that the threat he was scanning for was indifference. And, by his own report, Carlos was anything but indifferent to Jonathan – in his own words, "I'm crazy about him. Honestly, I can't believe I found someone like Jonathan to love me." At the same time, Carlos was very excited and passionate about his new job. He still loved and wanted Jonathan. However, his behavior was reminding Jonathan of his father's indifference, and Jonathan was protecting himself the best way he knew how, which was to turn his critical and attacking voice outwards at Carlos. For Carlos, criticism was the all-too-familiar threat for which *he* was scanning. When it got to be too much, Carlos would yell at Jonathan to stop picking on him. Jonathan would be reminded of his dad's criticism. As his other strategy was to try to bond with his critical father, he'd apologize and want to be soothed by or have sex with Carlos. This reminded Carlos of his mom's neediness. It was anything but a turn-on, and Carlos would distance himself even further, as he had with his mother to keep his sense of self intact.

In this example we can see that neither Jonathan nor Carlos was purposefully trying to hurt the other, but they were quickly losing the feeling of being on the same team. As they each started to experience the threat for which they were scanning in the relationship, they started to look at the other as the cause of their hurt and pain. They began unconsciously using the only defenses they knew—the defenses of a child. Each of them had started to think of the other as the enemy, as someone who was trying to purposefully hurt them.

We started out by helping Carlos and Jonathan empathize with each other by vulnerably sharing their histories and threats. Carlos began to see that Jonathan's criticism was not a purposeful attack but a desperate and roundabout attempt to get Carlos to love him and go back to giving him the attention that was so different from his father's neglect. Jonathan began to see that, far from being indifferent, Carlos just wanted to feel his own sense of confidence and worth by engaging in fulfilling work. This is a perfect example of the delicate balance that we all are trying to strike as we attempt to care for the relationship (attachment) and be true to ourselves (individuation). As Carlos moved more towards individuation, Jonathan feared that he was losing the attachment.

We helped Carlos and Jonathan understand that these shifts in the balance between attachment and individuation are not personal attacks or indicators that all is lost. Just knowing that it's not personal can relieve so much tension. In attempting to balance connection and selfhood you are bound to trigger your partner's past wounds and defenses. Additionally, just by being your beautiful, wonderful self, without trying at all, you will inevitably step on your partner's triggers. The more you can empathize with your partner instead of getting defensive, the more the two of you will feel you are on the same team. When your partner is hurt by something you do, take a deep breath, remember it is not about you, remind yourself that you are a good person and that your partner just feels hurt or sad sometimes, and see if you can empathize instead of defending.

As we worked with Jonathan and Carlos, helping them to use their histories to see and understand the reactions of their hurt inner children, it was as though lightbulbs went on in their minds. One of their main resources as a couple was humor and, by remembering their love for each other and looking at the fears of their inner children with compassionate humor, they were able to start to come back together and look at their problems as something that they could address as a team.

When Carlos realized how much Jonathan's behavior was reminding him of his mother, he laughed out loud. "Wow, Jon, you really don't look like my mom, but you do have that beautiful, dramatic flair she has – just one of the millions of reasons I fell in love with you." Together we came up with ways that Carlos could give Jonathan some attention without exhausting himself too much and that Jonathan could stop criticizing, instead bringing humor in as a resource. In one session Jonathan said, "Now when Carlos gets home looking like a dead man, I tickle him and say, 'Hey, Daddy, maybe tonight I can help you build your model airplanes.'"

Exercise: *Why I Want YOU on My Team*

It can be very helpful in getting back on the same team to begin by writing about or sharing the many reasons you chose to team up with this person in the first place. This will help you identify the positive resources each of you brings to the relationship. There are many ways you can do this exercise. One of our favorites is to write a love letter to your partner telling them all the things that made you decide to team up with them. You can also take some time to sit in person, look in each other's eyes, and tell each other everything that inspired you to make the commitment to be together.

Thanks to two of our clients, who agreed to have their letter printed, we are able to share one of our favorites with you:

Dear Sam,

First of all, you know that I'm extremely shallow, so I would never have teamed up with you if you hadn't been so crazy hot. Second, you completely accepted my shallowness and remembered to tell me how gorgeous I was at least 20 times a day. But seriously, when I think about what made me team up with you in the first place, it was the way that I felt when you held me in your arms and looked down at me with those huge brown eyes. I felt so safe and loved and accepted. I keep coming back to that word, 'accepted.' I think that is something that I had been missing my whole life. I always felt different or weird, but for some reason you seemed to enjoy everything that was weird about me and I stopped hiding and started being proud of who I am.

When I thought about having children with you, I thought, my kids are going to be held in those arms and looked at with those eyes and accepted for exactly who they are. I feel like you treat the people in your life with that same acceptance, and so you have brought me more of a feeling of family than I ever knew. Somehow people just stick to you like glue – which I guess I can understand, cause I kinda think of myself as the bubblegum that you'll never be able to get out of your hair. I also teamed up with you because of your ridiculous sense of humor. Even when I am at my crabbiest and bitchiest, somehow you get around it and can still make me laugh. You make me laugh at everything, including myself.

And then there are the little things, the hot pack you bring me when I'm PMSing, the way you sing in the shower like a complete idiot, and the fact that after six years of marriage and eight years of being together you still come around to my side of the car and open the door for me (also ridiculous in the best of ways).

I know things have been rough lately, but I also know that I can't imagine having anyone better on my team.

Love,

Your Slinky Cat, Amy

In the following chapters we will offer you a number of tools to help you get back on the same team.

Use Connection Tools

It is really helpful for you and your partner to have a language around triggers and connection so that you can know where you both stand in any given moment. To do this you can use one or both of the following tools or you can create your own shared tool that has resonance for both of you.

The Connect-O-Meter: The Connect-O-Meter is a scale of how connected you feel to your partner at any given moment, from zero to ten. If you are feeling no connection whatsoever, you are a zero on the scale; if you are bubbling over with a feeling of connection and closeness, you are a ten. The amount of connection fluctuates in every relationship, and this is normal. There are times in the relationship when you may have less of a sense of connection because each of you is doing your own activity, or you may still feel very connected even when you are not in direct contact.

When you are triggered, you may feel less connected or, if your partner is really there and available to you, you might feel triggered and connected at the same time. It is certainly unrealistic to expect that you will be at a ten all the time, but when you feel lower on the Connect-O-Meter, that is a good time to check in with yourself and see what you need in order to feel more connected. Sharing with your partner when you feel lower on the scale can also be useful. It can help them understand and empathize with you and give them a heads-up if you are feeling a strong lack of connection. *Don't forget* to also bring up positive moments and express appreciation of how close and loving you are feeling. For example, you could say, "I'm a perfect ten on the Connect-O-Meter right now. I really love it when you take a few minutes to look in my eyes. It feels so great!"

The Trigger Richter Scale: The Trigger Richter Scale is a reading of how triggered you are. A zero is when you are feeling neutral and fine. You might feel emotional when your Trigger Richter Scale is at zero, but you are not having the fight, flight, or freeze response. For example, you may be sad and crying but not feel urgent, fearful, or out of control. A ten feels like you are going to die – when animals or people have a fight, flight, or freeze response, they are meant to take some kind of self-preserving action, and people rarely get to a ten without doing something drastic.

To find your Trigger Richter Scale number, check in and see how you are feeling in your body. If there is some tension in your stomach or chest but it's not too bad, you might be at one or two. If you feel your heart racing and thoughts rushing out of control, you might be at five. If you feel like you want to break up the relationship or do something very destructive, you might be at eight or nine. Letting your partner know that you are triggered at a lower level on the scale, before things get too drastic, can help each of you attend to the triggering instead of continuing to fight or shut the other person out. It is also a way to take better care of yourself by helping others know what is going on inside you.

***

Journal opportunity: Triggers and Habits
Try keeping a journal of your triggers and your habitual responses to them.

Vote for Connection Instead of Protection

Once you have learned to recognize your triggers and know when you are in a triggered state, it is time to practice doing something else in those moments. We call this voting for connection instead of protection. Vulnerability is the best antidote to defensive protection, and the inner child is ultimately longing for the intimacy that comes from being vulnerable. When you are in protection mode, you are protecting the tender, beautiful, and precious parts of yourself. The problem with protecting your vulnerable parts is that it is precisely these parts that connect you to the people you love and help them connect to you. When your partner sees your soft, vulnerable parts, they are more likely to feel empathy. This will help them feel closer to you, comfort you, listen to you, and be responsive to your needs.

It can be very challenging to share yourself vulnerably. As a culture, we are taught that vulnerability and weakness are the same thing, which means people are often ashamed of their vulnerable parts. This is especially true for men, who are given the strong message that sharing their feelings or challenges is weak. Men are told to "man up" and get over their problems on their own. Whether you are a man or a woman, when you do open yourself up and someone responds poorly, it can be very painful and you might feel hurt or rejected.

To share vulnerably instead of defensively means talking directly and openly about your feelings, your desires, and your capacities, even if you are ashamed of some of them or wish they were different.

When Stephanie met Carl, she felt she had found her dream man, someone who was extremely attentive to her feelings but also able to stay strong in any crisis. She thought of him as her rock. After all, he was a soldier and, just like her own father, a real "man's man." What she loved most about Carl was that, no matter where they were, she always felt totally protected. She felt that way for the first five years of their relationship, until he came back from his second tour in Afghanistan with severe PTSD. He was suffering interrupted sleep from terrible nightmares and, during the day, out of nowhere, he would burst into tears. To protect Stephanie, he refused to share all of the atrocities he'd seen; he would simply lie next to her wanting her to hold him as he wept.

In the face of Carl's emotions, Stephanie was also inconsolable. She was completely turned off by what she perceived as Carl's weakness. She had no experience being with a man who was vulnerably sharing his feelings. Carl would have done anything to just shut his feelings down, and he felt hurt and rejected by Stephanie's disgust at them.

Carl reached out for some helpful trauma therapy at his local VA hospital, where he was able to share his experiences with someone who could relate and understand. He still cried at times but, even through his tears, he was able to communicate with Stephanie. Slowly but surely, Stephanie started to realize that Carl's emotions didn't mean he'd never be able to be strong and protect her, and she started to feel connected to him again. It was a long time before she was able to feel attracted to Carl and want sex with him again, but we will revisit the sexual aspects of their relationship later on in the book.

When you make room for your vulnerability and empathize with your partner's feelings, you begin to be on the same team again. While we would never wish the trauma of war on anyone, in some ways, having no choice but to show his feelings to Stephanie transformed Carl's terrible experience into a way to connect and strengthen the relationship. They learned that everyone has feelings and that these are the glue of relationships.

Learn the Tools of Vulnerability

Now that you know it is essential to be vulnerable in order to have deeply fulfilling relationships, you need to learn how to practice vulnerability on a day-to-day basis. Practicing vulnerability means knowing and sharing your feelings, needs, and boundaries with your partner. In order to do this, you need to know what each of these is. Once you have learned to recognize and accept them, you must learn how to communicate them vulnerably so that your partner can understand and accept them as well. To do this, you will need working definitions of "feeling," "desire," and "capacity" and "boundary." As this is a book for couples or people seeking a relationship, we will define these words specifically as they pertain to your relationship with your current or future partner.

What Is a Feeling?

Within a relationship, a feeling is what you experience in response to something your partner says or does (including nonverbal cues) or doesn't say or do. Examples of feelings are being hurt, elated, scared, excited, angry, loved, or frustrated. If you are not used to sharing your feelings vulnerably, or even knowing what they are, it can be helpful to search online for a list of feeling words and see how many feeling options are out there. While some people might report feeling anxious, we think of anxiety as an "anti-feeling," a way to stay away from underlying feelings that you don't want to feel, such as shame, fear, or grief.

Your feeling responses are not universal; they are personal. The way you react to your partner's words or actions will be different from how they would react to your saying or doing the same thing. Your feeling reactions are based on your own personal history. You cannot evaluate them based on some generic idea of what is or is not reasonable. We tell our clients that every emotional response is reasonable and logical based on their own personal history. If you were physically or emotionally abandoned by your parents, for example, it is reasonable to fear abandonment, even if in the present moment you are not being abandoned.

In relationships, feeling responses are a combination of present-moment feelings about your partner and how you felt in the face of similar circumstances in the past. Generally, when you have a strong emotional response to something your partner does, especially if it feels like an "overreaction," much of that response is not due to the current interaction. Your response is a mixture of your current feelings and your hurt inner child's feelings. We can't emphasize enough that you never have to check whether or not your feeling response is reasonable; if you are having it, it is reasonable in response to what is happening now *combined* with your own personal history. But this also means you are likely not seeing the person in front of you; you are reacting to the ways you were hurt in the past and missing the opportunities for connection that are here in the present.

It can be helpful to measure how much of your response is due to the present moment. Simply stating or acknowledging that your feelings are only partially a reaction to the current situation can help you bring your awareness and compassion to your inner child. This awareness also differentiates you from your inner child, so that you can take a more adult action.

In our work, we hear a lot of people say that they are "too sensitive." They believe this to be a negative quality and fear that others will judge them. We want to emphasize that *everyone is very sensitive* and that this is a wonderful part of being human. Some people have ways of protecting themselves that cause them to disconnect from their sensitivities, and some of these ways are socially acceptable, particularly for men. For example, not crying when you are hurt or emotionally or physically is thought of as being strong. You never lose your sensitivity; it just gets repressed, which can lead to disconnection, depression, harmful self-soothing practices, etc. If you stay connected or reconnect with your sensitivity, you can experience all of amazing intimacy your relationship has to offer.

Watch for Nonverbal Cues

Whether or not you are aware of it, you are constantly reading the nonverbal cues of your partner. Research suggests that sixty to ninety percent of our communication is nonverbal. We find this to be particularly true for couples who have been in their relationship for a while. Once you know someone well, you read and respond to every one of their little twitches, facial movements, body movements, tones of voice, etc.

While you are certainly reading your partner's cues, usually you are not doing this with any conscious awareness, so instead of noticing your responses, you simply react. By developing the skill of consciously witnessing your partner's nonverbal cues, you will be able to tell whether your partner is triggered. You can also observe your knee-jerk reactions to your partner's nonverbal cues. Once you have some awareness that you are affected by your partner's nonverbal cues, you can begin to bring in more deliberate responses instead of simply reacting. In later sections we offer you some positive communication tools that will help you respond in these moments with vulnerability and connection instead of protection.

For now, simply notice the following kinds of nonverbal cues to which you may be reacting: eye contact or lack thereof; body tension; body posture; breath (breathing or holding breath);

proximity (how close to or far from you your partner is); touch (whether or not and where your bodies are touching, or the quality of touch, such as firm or soft); and voice, including loudness and tone or attitude (sarcastic, hurt, angry). In order to know when you or your partner is in distress, you will want to get a baseline reading of the body. For example, some people hold their bodies with some tension even at their most relaxed, and some people speak loudly or quietly and it has nothing to do with how they are feeling. If you've been with your partner for a while, you will generally be able to tell when their nonverbal cues change from baseline to distressed or from baseline to joyful and connected. One couple with whom we worked, Scott and Alice, has a lot to teach us about the power of nonverbal cues.

Scott and Alice were an adorable young couple in their early twenties who came in to work on their sexual connection. We noticed a big disconnect in their communication. Alice grew up in a very kind, supportive, and highly conflict-avoidant family. Her family spoke in gentle voices with one another and, when there was a problem between any two members of the family, they had an unspoken rule that they should apologize quickly for what they'd done wrong and move on.

Scott grew up in a rough neighborhood, as had his parents and grandparents. As a result of their surroundings, his family had to be tough, and their communication style followed suit. They spent a lot of time in different rooms, yelling across the house to one another, and when there was a disagreement, they yelled at each other until someone backed down and "lost" the fight. Sometimes the boys would work out conflict through physical fights.

When Alice and Scott had a problem, Alice felt like most everything was her fault. She would put on her sweetest, most accommodating facial expression and, in a timid voice, attempt to gently apologize to Scott. The more kind, soft, and apologetic Alice's cues were, the more aggravated Scott got that she was not meeting him. Scott felt unseen and adopted his familial strategy of getting bigger. He would stomp around the house, yell, punch a wall – anything at all to get more of a reaction out of Alice. As Scott got louder, Alice resorted to her conflict-avoidant strategy and grew softer and quieter.

In their day-to-day interactions they were constantly triggered by each other's baseline and nonverbal cues. Scott always felt like Alice was scared of him or hiding some resentment, and Alice was constantly overwhelmed by Scott's boisterousness. Even when he was happy and jovial, she felt a bit overwhelmed by his loud voice and his highly expressive facial movements. Scott felt like he was being judged for being too aggressive, and Alice felt hurt that Scott thought she was a wimp.

In order for Scott and Alice to support and regulate each other's nervous systems, Scott learned to speak in a somewhat softer voice. If he wanted to punch something, he would warn Alice so she could decide whether she wanted to stay and be with him or take a walk. Alice learned to not take Scott's louder expressions so personally and to engage more directly with her own anger by saying things like "I'm really pissed off at you right now." Much to Alice's surprise, this made Scott feel safer. He felt like he could trust that she would tell him how she felt in a direct manner. In our sessions we practiced having Scott get more upset or animated while Alice worked on breathing and looking at him to see with her adult self that there was no real threat. She could see that he just needed to express himself.

Scott and Alice's example is a reminder that growing up in a family is like growing up in your own unique culture. In order to get along in your current relationship, you need to accept that your partner's ways of being, expressing, and understanding the world will be different from yours. As long as there is no abuse, there is no right way to behave or respond; there are just ways that are more compatible and easier to understand because they are more familiar. This is why it is important to learn your partner's baseline without judgment. That way, if you see an increase in body tension or see your partner holding their breath with downcast eyes, or if you ask your partner how they are and they snap back at you, curtly, "I'm fine," you know that they may be in some kind of distress. You may also notice your own bodily reactions to their nonverbal cues. When they pull away physically, do you get anxious and try to get closer, or do you pull away too?

Exercise: Read Your Partner's Nonverbal Cues
Take a moment with your partner to play with different kinds of nonverbal cues and pay attention to how you react to them.

Have one person be the giver of nonverbal cues and the other the receiver. As the giver, you will give the cues and notice what it feels like to give each of them. The receiver simply receives the cues and observes their own reactions. Go slowly, so that you have enough time to feel your responses. Notice your emotional responses and your physiological responses. Take turns being the giver and receiver and share your reactions.

1. Smile at your partner.
2. Give your partner a disapproving look.
3. Cross your arms and turn your gaze away from your partner.
4. Reach out to your partner like you want to give them a hug.
5. Say, "I'm fine," in a tone that lets your partner know that you don't mean it.
6. Touch your partner on their knee.
7. Scoot away from your partner.
8. Scoot closer to your partner.
9. Say something in a loud, angry voice to your partner, even just "I'm really angry."
10. Say something in a very quiet, accommodating voice to your partner, like "I'm really sorry."

Now that you can spot some of these nonverbal emotional cues, you can keep your eye out for those that indicate distress. When you see distress, you will need to switch from the regular rules of day-to-day conversation to much more specific and helpful rules that are useful for a challenging conversation. Before learning those rules, however, you need to know what the important ingredients are for these kinds of conversations. We have already been talking about how you can pay attention to the emotions that are present in your interactions with your partner. Additionally, you will need to know about your own and your partner's needs, capacities and boundaries.

Journal opportunity: Non-Verbal Cues and Triggers
Make a list of the non-verbal cues your partner makes that trigger you and write empathetically about what might make them do this. For example, "My partner sometimes looks away when they are talking to me. Maybe they feel overwhelmed by both looking in my eyes and trying to formulate their thoughts at the same time. Maybe they get worried about hurting my feelings so they need to focus away from me for a moment.

What Is a Need/Desire?

In a relationship, a need or desire is something that you want for yourself or that you want to happen. We do not differentiate between needs and desires but think of them as interchangeable. Sometimes couples will argue about whether something is a "need" or a "desire," usually valuing needs as more essential and desires as a luxury. But certain needs or desires might be essential for one person and not for another. We want to avoid any implication that there is a hierarchy in terms of how essential different needs are, so we will use the terms "need" and "desire" interchangeably.

Some common needs that you might have of your partner include physical affection, sex, emotional support, eye contact, shared parenting, financial support, honesty, monogamy or non-monogamy, shared interests/activities, time together, words of attraction or appreciation, and sharing of chores.

All children are full of needs. Depending on how they were dealt with in your family, you have developed a particular relationship to them. You may have been given everything you wanted and therefore feel a sense of entitlement. You may have gotten very few of your needs met, so you feel your needs strongly, are ashamed of having them, and may also judge your partner for having them. You may have gotten very little and shut down your connection with your needs, so you don't even really know what they are. These different ways to relate to needs can have big consequences for your relationship, so identifying your history with and relationship to needs is crucial.

Difficulties in relationships arise when needs are unmet, unexpressed, judged, or ignored. To have a great relationship it is important that each of you remember that everyone has needs and both your and your partner's needs are beautiful. When you honestly and directly express your needs, your inner child has the feeling of having an advocate out in the world, a feeling that it is okay to want what you want, regardless of whether you get it. It is also essential to accept that you will not get every one of your needs met by your partner or in life in general.

While they will not all be met, expressing your needs to someone who will listen to them and celebrate them without judgment is an enormously healing experience. What's more, expressing your needs exponentially increases the chances that they will be met. And finally, allowing yourself to feel disappointment without shutting down when your needs are not met is an enormously healing experience. (We will talk much more about disappointment in Part 2 of this book.) In order to have a flourishing relationship, you will need to know what you want, accept it, and communicate it to your partner. You will also need to hear, accept, and support your partner when they express their needs, whether or not you are able to meet them.

Turn Up the Volume on Your Desire

When someone asks you what you want, do you freeze up? Does your mind go blank? It may be that somewhere along the line you learned that many, if not most, of your desires were not going to be met. Instead of feeling the constant frustration and disappointment of not having them met and possibly even feeling guilty for having them in the first place, you learned to turn down the volume on your desires. But no one is able to completely shut down their needs. If you learned to disconnect from your desires because they were not met, not allowed, or even shamed, you might experience negative consequences including anxiety, depression, resentment, addiction, overindulgence, frustration, and anger.

When someone asks you what you want, do you feel angry, suspicious, or embarrassed? Somewhere along the line you may have learned that your desires were bad or shameful. A good number of them may have been met, but at a price – you were made to feel guilty or your desires were treated with disgust and rejection. When a child's desire is not met, they do not blame their parents. They can't, because their parents are responsible for their survival. Instead, when a child wants something and that desire is not met, they see their desires as bad and, eventually, themselves as bad for having the desire in the first place.

Perhaps when you asked your parents for what you wanted, they snapped at you to stop being so selfish. Or maybe they heaved a deep sigh and, with a pained expression, gave it to you, but then later you overheard them complaining that they didn't have any time for themselves or were running out of money because they were so busy doing or buying everything for you. You might have gotten the feeling that you shouldn't want what you want or that you always want too much. You might have learned to stop asking for attention or support or the shiny new toy that your friend had. You might have decided that you could get anything you needed on your own and given up depending on others.

None of this is to blame parents; it is very likely that your parents received the same messages from their parents or that, in the hustle and bustle of daily life, they didn't take the time to really consider what they could or could not give you. It is a rare parent who celebrates their child's desires and then sets appropriate boundaries without creating any guilt or shame. Just imagine a child taking away another child's toy. Some parents might slap their child for doing something like this. Others might scold the child or say, "That's not your toy. Give it back."

Can you imagine a parent saying, "Yes, sweetheart, I know that you really want Kelly's toy and it would be super fun to play with, but it is hers and you need to give it back to her. After you give it back, you can ask her if she would be willing to share it with you for a while." This parent is celebrating and supporting their child's desires while teaching them how to get along with a friend, but again, with the pace and frustrations of daily life, this kind of parenting is rare or, at the very least, inconsistent.

Know What You Want

When we invite people to explore their desires, most try to figure out with their brain what they want. The problem with this is that your brain is constantly filtering information through acquired beliefs about right and wrong. For example, if you think to yourself, "Mmm...I want a bag of chocolate chip cookies," your brain might also say, "You aren't supposed to have cookies before dinner" or "They will make you fat" or "Stop being so greedy." This is because your brain works through argument and debate. You can always think of a reason why you should or shouldn't want something, and your brain will talk you into and out of things a thousand times a day. Your body and your feelings, however, do not lie.

Here is one way to begin to turn up the volume on your desires. When you have any kind of decision to make, no matter how mundane, ask your body what it needs instead of your brain. It might take a while for you to begin to distinguish the voice of your body from the voice of your brain. For example, your brain might continue to say, "Yeah, I really want a bag of cookies," but your body might say, "I do want cookies right now, before dinner, but I actually only want two. I love the taste of chocolate on my tongue, but my stomach hurts when I have too many."

Next time you have any kind of decision to make, instead of going into a mental debate, take a few deep breaths, close your eyes, and visualize choosing each of the options in turn. We can use the cookies as an example. Imagine eating a cookie, chewing it, the flavor you get in your mouth, the way your body feels when you eat it. Notice the energy in your body, your mood, and your feeling of aliveness. Now imagine eating something else instead, and go through the same visualization process.

See which of your visualizations feels more uplifting, interesting, exciting, pleasurable, and self-affirming. It might sound silly when talking about food, but it's not. Every time you listen to your inner voice of desire, no matter how big or small, you affirm that you are important and that your desires deserve attention and consideration. Don't wait for or expect anyone else to know your desires if you aren't willing to take the time to do so yourself. You may find that a cookie sounds absolutely scrumptious and let yourself have the pleasure, or you may find that your body actually wants something else. The most important part is that you listen to and honor your desires in a way they may not have been honored in the past.

Exercise: Celebrate Your Desires

You can do this by yourself, with a friend, with a coach or therapist, or with your partner. Whether you are doing it on your own or with a supportive person, make sure that you do it in such a way that you feel safe to acknowledge all of your desires. Sit in front of the mirror or face to face with your support person. This can be just for you, or you can take turns and each of you can practice celebrating your own and each other's desires.

By yourself: Start out by closing your eyes and letting yourself feel a list of all of your desires in your life around work, family, sex, intimacy, anything really – maybe one of them is a desire to have a pet. It doesn't matter at all what the desires are; they may even be impossible desires or contradictory desires, desires that it would be impossible to have all at once, like "I want to spend time with my best friend right now and I also want to be alone." You can want both of those at the same time without being able to have them. This exercise is not about getting anything, just about celebrating what you want. Allow yourself to really want everything that you want and feel these desires and longings in your body. Say all of your desires out loud. Once you have said them aloud, then say aloud to yourself, "All of my desires are beautiful." Go through this a few times, closing your eyes, feeling your longing, and then repeating, "All of my desires are beautiful."

With a supportive person: As above in the "by yourself" exercise, start by closing your eyes and feeling all of your desires. Allow yourself to feel the longing and the beauty of all of those desires. When you open your eyes, you can say all of your desires aloud to the other person or simply feel the desires and open your eyes. Your supportive person then says, "All of your desires are beautiful." Go through this a few times, closing your eyes, feeling your desires, and then opening your eyes and having your supportive person say, "All of your desires are beautiful."

Notice what happens inside you as you feel, share (if you are comfortable doing so), and celebrate all of your desires. Notice what happens inside your body. Do you feel less tension or more tension? Do you feel excited, sad, frightened, motivated? Take a moment and share what you feel like and then, if you are taking turns, switch and allow the other person to share and have their desires celebrated and accepted.

Journal opportunity: Celebrating Desires
Make a list of all of the desires that you celebrated so that you can begin to ask for what you want in all of your relationships.

Ask for What You Want
Once you have accepted your desires, it is essential to ask for what you want. This is not about being selfish, just about honoring your

selfness. Your selfness is the holistic experience and expression of your being, which includes your emotions, capacities, and desires. In order to bring yourself fully into intimacy, you need to express all of these aspects of yourself. In a relationship, you might not feel a right to your desires and you also may not feel a sense of safety in expressing them, for fear of rejection or of hurting your partner.

If you are like most people, you define success by what you get instead of by the bravery of asking for it. However, the act of allowing yourself to want what you want and ask for it is the true success and deserves a tremendous amount of celebration. If you get what you asked for, that's a bonus. If you don't, then it is important to allow yourself to feel the feelings of rejection and disappointment that can come with not getting.

Success is defined not by getting what you want but by knowing you truly tried and were brave enough to ask. The act of asking for what you want is saying to yourself and your inner child, "My desires are important enough to go after" and "I am worth it." You are making yourself vulnerable to rejection because you are putting your true self out there. Yet you are also accepting of yourself in every moment, whether you are getting a "yes" or a "no," and this acceptance helps you move beyond shame, stay in touch with your desires, and continue to pursue them no matter what. It is the expression of your desires, not their fulfillment, that is the triumph.

When you express your desires in a relationship, your partner may feel threatened for many reasons. They may feel that they are supposed to give you what you want, or they may feel that they can't give it to you and get upset that you've asked. They may have grown up with the message that having desires means being spoiled and therefore feel that you want too much. Later in the book we will talk about how to create an honoring conversation so that you, as a couple, can make room to hear and celebrate each other's desires in a safe container that minimizes feelings of fear and rejection.

Teach People How to Love You

If you are like most people, you probably don't have any idea what you can request. There are so many unspoken beliefs and rules about what it is okay or not okay to ask for. In truth, you need to be able to ask for both attachment/connection needs and individuation/freedom needs. We all have needs in both of these categories.

The biggest roadblock to asking for what you want is the harmful, romantic myth "If they loved me, they would know what I want." It is the unfounded belief that if your partner is truly your soul mate, they will prove it by knowing exactly what you want and need all the time without your having to tell them. While there are many wonderful people out there with whom you can have a great relationship, not one of them will know what you need enough of the time. You will have to ask for what you want and teach them how to give it to you.

There are a couple of reasons for this. First, each person has their own particular needs and desires around love and intimacy. Second, those needs and desires change from day to day depending on your mood, what is happening in your life, and your emotional state. As you grow and change, so will your needs, and you will need to update your partner on those changes. "Yes, I know that I told you I didn't like my shoulders rubbed before sex, but that was before I had to carry around kids all day. Now it would really be a great way for me to transition from being the kid's dad to being your lover."

To really get the kind of love you want and to give your partner the love they want, you need to teach them how to love you and learn the particulars of how they want to be loved. You need to tell and teach them gently and kindly how you like to connect when you're sad or angry (for example, being held, listened to, or reassured) and what kinds of things let you know that you are loved (for example, words of appreciation, gestures, touch, or sex), and you will need to ask your partner what they want as well.

Don't assume that your partner has any idea what you want them to do for you or how to do it. It is also important to broaden your ideas of what you can ask for. Usually people think they can ask only for certain kinds of touch or specific actions. However, in order to teach someone how to love you, you will need to ask for things such as emotional reassurance or words of desire and appreciation. When teaching your partner how to love you, you will need to be very specific. "I need you to be more emotionally available" is not specific enough. Your partner will have no idea what you mean. You will need to say, "When you see that I'm sad, it would help me very much if you could take a break from what you are doing, sit down in front of me about this close, and look in my eyes. It would also help if you put a hand on my knee." Once you have told your partner what you want, demonstrate it by doing it to them, so that they get it. We find that people are especially uncomfortable asking for compliments or words of desire: "Tell me how sexy my ass looks in these jeans" or "Tell me how handsome I am right now."

If you feel like you have already asked your partner for something a million times, notice your tone of voice and how you are looking at them (or not looking at them) when you ask. If you are angry, hurt, or demanding, their brain will not be in a place where they can learn, because they will be anxious and triggered themselves. When a person is triggered, their frontal cortex is bypassed, so they are not capable of learning anything new. Even if you are asking very nicely and from a calm place, don't expect that you will have to tell them only once or that they will get it right the first time. Some people take a long time to learn a new skill and need many repetitions in order to learn. Some people will not be motivated or capable of learning everything that you want to teach them. This is not because they don't love you; they may feel like they are okay the way they are or just have trouble taking instructions. Later in the book we will talk more about what to do if your partner cannot offer you what you want.

Ask for Connection

The following are great ways to practice asking for what you want around connection and attachment.

Eye Contact

Eye contact is a powerful connection tool. It is an indicator that you are fully present with your partner and available for connection. The kind of eye contact you want will be different depending on the context. For example, you might want your partner to look at you with acceptance while you talk about your day but want them to look at you with desire when they are seducing you.

Exercise: Show Your Partner You Are There and You Want Them

Eye contact can convey many different messages. Two examples are "I'm here with you" and "I want you." Take a few minutes to explore the different experiences of conveying these two messages. "I'm here with you" eye contact means sitting with your partner and sending love, empathy, and understanding through your eyes. What many people don't realize is that the first step in "I'm here with you" is actually to connect with yourself. Take a moment to feel your feet on the ground, breathe into your belly and chest, and bring kindness, compassion, and curiosity to yourself. Next, look in your partner's eyes and share that feeling without feeling like there is anything else you need to do. You don't have to be nice or smile or try to make your partner feel anything. You are just being there with them exactly as you are and allowing them to be exactly as they are.

Now try to bring some desire into your eyes with the feeling "I want you." As with "I'm here with you," feel your connection with your own body, your breath, your cock or pussy, and your belly and chest. Let yourself connect with your authentic desire and then try projecting different attitudes of desire through your eyes. Try letting your desire be assertive – even demanding. Hold this feeling of "I want you" and try to communicate it through your eyes. Then let it become receptive; imagine inviting your partner into your body and receiving them fully. As you hold this feeling of receptivity, show it to your partner through your eyes.

Share Quality Time

Shared quality time is time that you spend with another person doing something that you or they or both of you find connecting and fulfilling. One of the biggest mistakes people make in attempting to create shared quality time in their relationship is to fall into a very limited cultural idea of what constitutes quality time. They will grudgingly schedule a date night, make a reservation at their usual restaurant, and then sit there eating and picking on each other about whether or not someone remembered to pay the mortgage.

Quality time is not about what you do; it is about how you do it. Really being there and being present in the experience is what quality time is all about. Which activities constitute shared quality time is different for everyone. It can be cuddling on the couch, cleaning out the closet, having sex, gossiping about your family of origin, going on a date night, vacationing, going on a walk, shopping, dancing, philosophizing, talking about your children, or anything that increases your feelings of love and attachment. Coming to these experiences with intention, asking for what you want out of the quality time, and teaching the other person how to give it to you are very important.

The first time you try to do one of these things together, you will need to ask for what you want and give feedback about how you feel. Don't expect the other person to engage in the experience exactly the way you want them to right away.

Let's take the example of Daria and Nicole's picnic. After talking about what they wanted to do for their shared quality time, they agreed that they loved picnics and decided to go the following Saturday. Right away, Daria started organizing for the picnic. She gathered the tablecloth, utensils, and special glasses in the perfect picnic basket. She consulted Nicole on each of the decisions that needed to be made – location, food, time of day, etc.

Every time Daria shared a new idea or asked a question about the picnic, Nicole got more irritated. It turned out that Nicole wanted to go on the picnic because it sounded like a really easy, relaxed way to get out of the house. On Saturday they would swing by the local grocery store, grab some snacks, throw a blanket down, and sprawl out. What she wanted more than anything else was a brainless break, while Daria wanted to create the perfect, special, romantic moment and considered consulting each other and preparing together part of the shared quality time. These kinds of misunderstandings happen all the time when couples first try to create shared quality time, so there needs to be space to iron out the differences and see, without judgment, what each person really needs from the experience.

Exercise: Define Your Quality Time

Step 1: Take some time to brainstorm activities or conversations you'd like to have during your shared quality time. Examples of activities might be dancing, revisiting romantic places from your history together, or taking a bike ride to some secluded place for a picnic. Some fun conversational topics might be "What experiences make you feel most spiritual or connected to yourself?" "What are your most recent dreams or visions for yourself in your life?" or "What is something you did as a child that made you feel happy, free, or playful?"

Step 2: Pick one of the items on your list and tell your partner your fantasy about how it might go. Where would it be? What would it look like? What would you talk about? What kind of touching would be involved? What do you want to feel? For example, you might hope that you feel relaxed, pampered, adored, adventurous, seen, enthusiastic, supported and understood, challenged, emotionally connected, etc.

Appreciate Your Partner

When you have been in a relationship with someone for a while and have lost some of the wondrous and shiny feelings of newness, you may begin to take many of the things your partner does for granted. Instead you begin to focus on what you want them to do differently. Part of being on a team is relying on another person to share all of the tasks, needs fulfillment, and emotional work of day-to-day life. When you depend on someone else, they won't always do things exactly the way you want them to, and recognizing that there are multiple "right" ways of doing something is very important for creating a strong, positive connection.

The bare minimum of appreciation is allowing people to help you in their own way and accepting their help as it is offered. Beyond this, you can nurture your relationship by taking the time to actually thank your partner for everything they do to make your day-to-day life together work – cooking a meal, bringing in a steady income, paying the bills, going to the market, washing the dishes. Even if it is their agreed-upon responsibility to do these things, it is still nice for your partner to hear how much they are appreciated once in a while. Simple words like "It means a lot to me that you take care of the cooking" or "God, I hate paying the bills. What would I do without you?" make a big difference.

There are also many rarely acknowledged tasks that people do in a relationship. For example, you might be the one in the relationship who usually reaches out after there is a fight, or your partner might be the one who always initiates sex. These are big relationship necessities and can be difficult to do because they mean risking rejection. These less-acknowledged tasks need to be seen and appreciated as well.

⌒

Exercise: Share Mutual Appreciation
Share with your partner the things that you appreciate about them. If your partner leaves something out that you'd really like to be appreciated for, gently and without scolding remind them of it.

Show Physical Affection
If it was not a big part of your family experience growing up, it is easy to forget to connect physically with your partner outside of sex. However, especially for some people, physical connection is essential to their sense of well-being. Spontaneous touch throughout the day and some physical connection before going to bed can be very relaxing and connecting.

Some people stop wanting to receive physical affection from their partner because they feel that they are getting it only when it is a prelude to sex and never "just because." It is very important to have physical connection throughout your life together that is part of the day-to-day flow and occasionally leads to sex. Other people avoid touching their partner for fear it means they are promising sex when they may just want to kiss or cuddle. Part of asking for what you need means telling your partner if you need to give or receive some touch that is not going to lead to sex.

There are many kinds of physical affection that you can give each other throughout the day and evening. These include hugs, cuddles, kisses, massage, stroking or petting, squeezes, bites, smelling each other, pats on the butt, hair caresses, and maybe a favorite of yours that we have left out. When you touch your partner, try to be conscious and aware so you don't end up doing "habitual touch" – mindless, disconnected, and repetitive touch that is more annoying to the body than relaxing, like stroking someone's arm up and down in the same place and at the same pace over and over again or patting them on the head like a puppy.

Exercise: Teach Your Partner Physical Affection
Take some time to talk with your partner about when and how each of you would like to be touched during the day and in bed. (We will talk much more in the next section about how to touch during sex.) For now, talk about the kinds of touch you like and demonstrate them by doing them to your partner the way that you like them to be done. It is very difficult to picture and learn what someone is telling you about touch without a good physical example. Also share with each other the kinds of touch that you don't like. For example, sometimes when people are concentrating on an

important task or trying to fall asleep, touch can be disruptive, so be respectful of your partner's needs and boundaries.

Dream Together

When you have been together as a couple for a long time, you may find that you spend your time talking about day-to-day needs and forget to talk about your deeper aspirations and the ways that you are growing and changing. Remember those all-night talks when you first met and were learning about each other? Twenty years in, you can still have those talks, especially if you look at your partner as someone who is unique and always growing and changing.

Take some time together to share and talk about your dreams. Talk about what you want for your career and for the two of you as a couple. Where do you want to travel? Where do you want to live? How many children do you want, if any, and how do you want your life to look when the children leave the nest? Instead of expecting that your partner will always be the same person they were when you married them, make room for the fact that you are both growing and changing over the years, and keep each other posted on those changes. Make special time to share your dreams and fantasies without doing any problem solving or talking about whether or not they are possible. When you let your imaginations soar together, you can directly face your fear of change and see your partner in a sexy new light.

Honor Your Freedom

In addition to the need for connection, you and your partner have a need for self-expression and the freedom to be who you are on your own terms. The following are some examples of individuation needs and ways to ask for them to best receive your partner's support.

The list of possible freedom needs is endless because there are so many ways people want to express themselves. Couples are constantly overtly and covertly negotiating these needs in a relationship. They can include bedtime and wake-up time, the amount of time to invest in work, which friends to have and how much time to spend with them individually and together, dietary choices, how much alone time to have, etc. Negotiating needs for freedom and self-expression is a challenging day-to-day task of relationships.

So often people do not ask directly for what they want, instead trying to get approval and acceptance from their partner in covert ways. One of our favorites, which we see all the time, is when one person wants something but asks the other person if they want it. Instead of saying, "I'm hungry" or "I want to spend more time with my friends," they say, "Are you hungry?" or "It seems like you aren't spending much time with your friends these days."

In order to teach your partner how to love you, it is very helpful to ask directly for what you need. It is also extremely important not to shame each other for your differences around these needs. For example, if you are the partner who needs more connection time, don't tell your partner, who needs more alone time, that they are "anti-social." People tend to shame and judge their partners for wanting things that scare them or make them unhappy and uncomfortable. They use all sorts of arguments, statistics, and studies to show that what they need or want to do is better than what their partner needs or wants to do. One early bird said to her night-owl husband, "They say every hour of sleep you get before midnight is worth two hours after midnight." She did not want to accept her partner's natural sleep cycle because she felt lonely waking up by herself in the morning and wanted him to share breakfast and her morning walk.

You will be most likely to get empathy, connection, and understanding if you share vulnerably when you want something different from what your partner wants. For example, the night owl could say, "I get my best work done at night, and I really feel alive and inspired to write and reach out to friends. I really love staying up late after everyone else is asleep because I get this quiet, alone time uninterrupted by the daytime noise." The early bird might say, "I totally get why you love staying up at night. Sadly, I can't even think after ten p.m., and I really miss taking walks with you after our morning coffee. I wish we could get up early together." Oftentimes, when people really listen and empathize instead of shaming, or make room for their partner's disappointment without trying to fix it or argue that they shouldn't be disappointed, they will find more generosity for a middle ground. We will go into detail on how to deal with disappointment in Part 2.

Exercise: Have a Desire-Honoring Conversation
Find a time when you and your partner are both feeling connected and supportive. Find a place where you can have uninterrupted privacy, eye contact, and physical touch. Remember that this is a non-judgmental conversation about a desire, and expressing a desire does not necessarily mean that it will be met. It is not your job to meet your partner's desire in this exercise but to listen with

empathy, support, and compassion and share your authentic feelings and fears about that desire.

We think it is best to take turns asking for what you want, so that you are dealing with one person's desire at a time. When your partner shares a desire, resist the temptation to share your counter-desire.

If you are the one sharing a desire, think of one desire you are afraid, or have in the past been afraid, to share with your partner. Once you have it in mind, notice what fears arise. Are you afraid that your partner will leave? That they won't be able to give it to you? That your even asking will make them scared or mistrustful? Do you feel like you don't deserve to have your desire met? Are you afraid your partner will think of you as selfish or shame or judge you or your desire?

Share your feelings and fears about sharing the desire and then ask for what you want in the most straightforward way possible. For example, you might say, "I want you to have rough sex with me."

As the listener, see if you can take a moment to celebrate your partner's desire as simply that, a desire and a beautiful part of who they are. Imagine their gaining a sense of self-expression and enjoyment from your fulfilling this desire, and see if you can say something to them in support of this, for example, "I can imagine that my having rough sex with you would be a huge turn-on and really exciting."

Now take a moment to notice what feelings and fears come up in the face of your partner's desire. You may have mixed positive and challenging feelings. Notice if you feel hurt, excited for your partner, angry, loving, appreciative that they've shared, rejected, uncertain, left out, afraid, etc. The person sharing the desire should take some time to really hear your feelings and tell you what feelings they have in response. The two of you may need to do a couple of rounds of this.

Now, as the listener, check in with yourself about your capacity (see the section below on capacity) and share your conclusions with your partner. Are you willing to do growth work around your feelings and fears? If something isn't okay with you, you will need to be present and make room for your partner's disappointment.

Some examples of what you might say:

- "I don't want to do it, and I don't want you to do it with anyone else, but I'm here to hear your disappointment as much as you need to share it."
- "I'm not ready for you to do it right now, but I'm willing to work on my fears around it and see if I can grow and get comfortable. I will also need to learn what you mean by "rough sex" and might need to practice."
- "I don't want to bring in this roughness, but I'm okay with your going and getting it somewhere else. If you do that, I have the boundary that you...(do it with someone I can meet, do it with someone you aren't going to see again, use protection, etc.)."

This is an ongoing communication and negotiation – desires that give rise to big feelings and fears need to be heard and processed fully.

Now that you have a better idea of how to identify and ask for what you need, it is also important to be aware and accepting of your and your partner's capacity to give each other what you want.

What Is Your Capacity?

Capacity is a set of personal limits that each person has as a result of who they are and their life experiences so far. Regardless of what we want our capacity to be, each of us has our own limits. You know you are beyond your capacity when you feel overwhelmed, exhausted, reclusive, and/or demotivated. In order to talk about your capacity in a relationship, it is helpful to understand the concept more generally. Everyone has their own human capacities. For example, everyone can go only so long without eating or sleeping before they pass out, but the amount of time that this takes varies from person to person. You may spend a lot of your time comparing your capacity to others' and wishing yours was different.

Based on your own personal histories, you and your partner have certain physical and emotional capacities that limit what you can give each other. You know that you have hit your capacity when something that you are doing or that someone is doing to you feels physically or emotionally uncomfortable. Knowing your capacity is an imperfect process. There will be times when it is very obvious and other times when you won't even realize you are beyond your capacity until after it has happened.

Your capacities are not fixed and will change over time based on simple factors such as rest and exercise and more complex factors such as how connected you are feeling to yourself and your partner. Despite your best attempts, your capacity will not change through your pushing yourself to do or handle things you cannot. This is why we can't emphasize enough that it is important not only to recognize your own capacity and your partner's but also to accept and embrace your capacities without feeling that they are shortcomings. Having higher or lower capacity than your partner in some area doesn't make you better or worse than them.

When you stay within your capacity, you will feel at ease, connected, present, and motivated. If you push and push, you will end up getting yourself into situations where you are overwhelmed by constant triggering or resentment. If you keep pushing, over time you may get depressed, have panic attacks, lose your libido, lose attraction to your partner, lose interest in pursuing your life goals, be anxious or snappy all the time, eat emotionally, etc. It is important to know and honor your capacity while being open to finding out your limits and possible places to stretch and grow.

The following examples show how some of the couples you have met so far began to honor their own and each other's feelings, needs, and capacities in order to have more fulfilling and connected relationships.

In the example of Jack and Anne, Jack wished that he were fully capable of taking care of himself and hiding his depression from Anne, but he actually did not have the capacity to do this. He needed Anne's help and support when he was feeling sad. Instead of continuing to hide his sadness, he began to share his feelings vulnerably with Anne. This created more empathy and less dissociation on her part.

In Carlos and Jonathan's case, Jonathan was very ashamed of how much attention he needed from Carlos and was upset that he didn't have the capacity to go without that attion. When he got short and angry with Carlos, he was even angrier with himself for needing Carlos at all. Over time, he began to ask for attention in humorous or direct ways, accepting that it was beyond his capacity to go without attention and affection instead of trying to deny it. Carlos, for his part, had always been superhuman in his ability to work, get everything done, and take care of everyone. After his disability and the taxing experience of his new job, Carlos was ashamed to admit the limits of his capacity. He wasn't able to give Jonathan everything he needed all the time, and his capacity for giving Jonathan attention was lower than when they first met. When Carlos shared vulnerably about his lowered capacity and his shame about it, Jonathan saw how badly Carlos wanted to meet his needs and felt empathy for Carlos, as well as feeling very loved and cared for. When you honor and share your capacity, your partner may be able to see that you are not meeting their needs isn't something personal against them; you have simply bumped up against the limits of your capacity.

Accept Your Capacity

Depending on your personal history and beliefs, accepting your capacity may be a big challenge. Some of us grow up being taught and believing the old adage, "When the going gets tough, the tough get going." In your family of origin or community, having a "thick skin" or "buckling down" and getting through life may have been the ideal, and if you showed any weakness or admitted you felt challenged, you would be emotionally ripped apart. You may have learned to hide feelings of being overwhelmed by dissociating or distancing.

Admitting that you cannot actually handle something can be very painful. When you acknowledge that continuing on the same path or putting up with something you've put up with is actually debilitating to you in some way, you may judge yourself harshly and beat yourself up for being "weak" or a "failure."

Once you move beyond the pain and self-judgment of feeling weak or like a failure, great rewards come from accepting your capacity. The first is a sense of freedom from the burden of trying to handle something that you can't while staying connected to yourself and those you love. When you admit your capacity and stop pushing yourself beyond it, you are able to be real and connected with the people you love.

What Are Boundaries and Why Do You Need Them?

Once you have acknowledged your capacity, it is essential to set boundaries in your relationship so as to avoid exceeding your capacities. Boundaries are what you communicate to your partner about your personal limits in the relationship. You can use your knowledge about your capacity to decide what boundaries you want to set.

In addition, you can also set boundaries when you don't want to do something even if it would not be beyond your capacity. It is ok to give yourself room to breathe and not push yourself to be right up at the edge of your capacity all the time. In this way, boundaries do not need to be justified or explained, they just are. It is important to notice, however, if you are setting boundaries that have nothing to do with your capacity for some other reason like being angry at your partner. For example, you might set the boundary that you don't want to have sex during the week and the real reason you are setting it is because you are frustrated that you not getting help with the kids when your partner comes home from work. In a case like this, it will be better to communicate your feelings than to set a retaliatory boundary.

Keeping your boundaries is essential to the intimacy and longevity of a relationship because they help you create trust and prevent resentment. Knowing your capacities and sharing your boundaries with your partner creates a situation where your partner can trust that you will take good care of yourself. If you take good care of yourself, you will not build resentment or shut down. When you allow your boundaries to be crossed in a relationship, and especially when you do it over and over again, you begin to build resentment and distance from the person with whom you want to be closest.

One example of a place you might have a boundary in a relationship is in how much you are willing to listen to your partner vent. One day, you might be feeling relaxed and curious and have plenty of capacity to listen. Three days later, you might have had a terrible day, and when your partner starts to vent, you realize that listening is making you feel frustrated and annoyed.

It may be very important for you to set boundaries when you are not certain what your desires and capacities are in a given situation and need some room to find out. Our clients Suze and Allen are a great example. On her wedding day, Suze's mother had taken her aside and told her, "When it comes to sex, you probably won't like it, but it's your job to make sure your husband is sexually satisfied. I have never once said no to my husband." Needless to say, this was a confusing message, because there were times when Suze did enjoy sex, but she felt like she wasn't supposed to, and often she had sex with Allen thinking that it was her obligation.

If there is one truth that we have learned about sex from all of our work with couples, it's that there is nothing sexy about "obligation sex." Because Suze was having so much obligation sex, her own authentic desire for sex began to fade, and by the time they came to us, Suze and Allen were in a mostly sexless marriage. When they did have sex, Allen could tell that Suze wasn't interested at all, and this made him feel like a perpetrator. He started to avoid sex, though he missed it terribly and felt very rejected. Eventually, both Suze and Allen were avoiding almost all physical intimacy.

In one of their first sessions, we told Suze that she had a right to pleasure and that it was not her job to have sex with Allen. We told her that, if she didn't want to, she never had to have sex with Allen again. This radical idea, so different from the message she had received from her own mother, finally allowed Suze to see that she had not even allowed herself to learn her desires and capacities in regards to sex, let alone share her boundaries with Allen. As a result, she had been angry and blamed Allen for crossing unstated boundaries; she had wanted Allen to know when she didn't want sex without her having to tell him.

Through our work with her, Suze realized that because she believed she did not have a right to boundaries around sex, she allowed her boundaries to be crossed over and over again. There was no way for Allen to know this without her telling him. When she realized this, and that she could tell Allen when she wanted sex and when she didn't, she started to feel empowered instead of obligated. This also allowed her to realize that there were times when she authentically wanted sex. As she started respecting her own boundaries and feeling empowered to communicate them, her innate desire had room to breathe, grow, and find its own expression.

Know When You Are Letting Your Boundaries Be Crossed

Experiencing anger or the physical sensations of shutting down, dissociating, or feeling queasy are good signs that you are letting someone cross your boundaries. Please notice that we are saying not that someone is crossing your boundaries but that you are *letting* your boundaries be crossed. People allow their boundaries to be crossed all the time in relationships because they are afraid they will be left or will hurt their partner. Unfortunately, trying to avoid loss or hurt by allowing your boundaries to be crossed over and over again actually kills intimacy, which is much more likely to lead to loss and hurt in the long run. Remember, unless someone is physically forcing you, emotionally abusing you, or intimidating or blackmailing you, they are not crossing your boundaries; you are letting your boundaries be crossed.

It is your personal responsibility to pay attention to your boundaries and to care for them by communicating them when necessary. No one can know your boundaries but you. If you expect others to track them and protect them, you will experience a tremendous amount of disappointment and it will be difficult to have a healthy relationship. The good news is that it is possible to learn your boundaries and share them in ways that are both clear and loving. To avoid conflict in your relationship, begin noticing when you are allowing your boundaries to be crossed.

When we first started working with Suze, it was very difficult for her to tell when she authentically wanted some sexual connection and when she was forcing herself to have sexual experiences that did not feel good to her. Suze's mother had not only told her that she would not like sex but also spent decades engaging in "obligation sex," and Suze's father presumably hadn't noticed or cared enough to do anything about it. She had witnessed and experienced the poor connection her parents had as a result. Having grown up in this home and in a society that does not champion women's sexual development and autonomy, Suze often didn't even register her own positive feelings of arousal. She would often approach sexual experiences by shutting down to get through them. As we worked to sensitize the inner voices of her desire and boundaries and to help her notice when she was shutting down, she began to get a sense of when she actually wanted sexual connection and to appreciate what was in it for her.

Fear of loss makes setting boundaries an imperfect science. It was important for Suze to be gentle with herself and learn that she was entitled to institute a boundary despite having allowed it to be crossed in the past. When she did finally share already-crossed boundaries with Allen, at first he was shocked and hurt that she hadn't brought them up before. He felt sad, for example, that Suze had been enduring sex with him and felt like it was his fault. We worked with Allen to help him understand that Suze had been allowing her boundaries to be crossed because he was so important to her and she was afraid of losing him. We worked with Allen on ways to listen to her boundaries and still make passes at her and seduce her. Suze learned that sometimes it took her a while to get turned on, and that she could start a sexual interaction, see if she felt aroused, and then tell him whether she wanted to continue based on whether she was able to get into the experience after some warm-up.

Exercise: Offer a Boundary Lovingly

Boundaries are essential to love and intimacy, which makes offering a boundary a gift. You are trusting that your partner will listen and respect your boundaries and honestly letting them know what you need to feel relaxed and safe in the relationship. Unfortunately, when people share their boundaries, they often feel like they are being selfish or hurting their partner. Because of these fears, you may not share your boundaries in a clear way, or you may put off sharing them and build resentment. By the time you share your boundaries clearly, you are already angry or frustrated with yourself or your partner, and the boundaries come out sounding harsh. But if you remember that sharing a boundary is a huge gift to yourself, your partner, and the relationship, you can offer a boundary lovingly and joyfully.

Think of a boundary that you already have with your partner or one that you have not yet expressed, and try saying it from a place of love and joy. For example, you might say: "I feel much closer to you when we have sex when I feel like it. Tonight I'm not feeling like it because I need to be well rested in the morning," or "I really love hearing about your life, but I've had a rough day and I don't have the bandwidth to listen right now." While your partner might feel hurt or take some distance, it is better to allow them to experience their disappointment than for you to end up shut down and resentful. Shutting down and building resentment creates more hurtful disappointment and damage to the relationship in the long term.

Allen really did not want Suze to have sex when she wasn't feeling like it, and he was very supportive of her sharing her boundaries in any way she wanted. Eventually, Suze not only felt confident telling Allen when she didn't want to have sex but even learned to notice her own desire and occasionally initiated sex with Allen, which delighted him to no end.

Journal opportunity: Boundaries
Write about a time when you let your boundaries be crossed, the consequences of this and what you would have liked to have done differently.

Share Your Feelings, Needs, and Boundaries

Vulnerably sharing your feelings, needs, and boundaries is the gateway to emotional intimacy. At the beginning of a relationship, it is easy to share with your partner because most of what you are sharing is positive feelings of excitement, love, arousal, and happiness. Your partner's more annoying habits seem like cute idiosyncrasies. As you begin to really let the other person in and feel more attached to them, you begin to experience your fears and insecurities in the relationship. The little habits that seemed so cute at the beginning start to become more annoying, but you are much less likely to share feelings of insecurity, boundaries, or uncomfortable needs for fear of hurting your partner or creating distance.

Surprisingly, sharing these more challenging feelings, needs, and boundaries lays the foundation for trust, deeper intimacy, and growth in the relationship. In order to share in a way that will deepen intimacy rather than doing harm, you will need to learn the tools of emotional sharing. The first thing you need to be able to do is identify that you are in an emotional conversation.

A relationship involves a constant exchange of verbal and non-verbal information. If it is a decent relationship, most of this information exchange will have a neutral or positive emotional quality and effect. If it occasionally has a negative tinge, you probably can move through it and get back to a neutral or positive place without needing to address it. However, if you have moved into a more intense state of challenging feelings, it's time to switch gears and acknowledge that you are in an emotional conversation.

This is where most couples get stuck. They keep trying to have a "regular" conversation about facts and employing logic when the limbic system is activated and the emotions need attention. Until you realize that you are in an emotional conversation and attend to the emotions, you will probably continue to escalate negative feelings and feel like your partner is antagonistic and eventually the enemy. In order to create intimacy and trust and be able to share your feelings with your partner, you need to recognize that you are having an emotional conversation and learn how to listen. You will need to listen to your partner's hurt inner child and their upset adult. You will also need to share your feelings vulnerably so as to engender empathy and support. You will need to avoid communication pitfalls that create an atmosphere of blame, shame, or alienation, and you will need to listen to the emotions underneath the words that your partner is saying. By doing all this, you can create a positive emotional feedback loop of mutual support, love, connection, and growth.

Remember, *you will not do this perfectly*. When you read a self-help book, it is easy to get into the mind-set that you will get to a place where all of this is easy and you have a perfect relationship without any conflict. This is completely unrealistic. You are human, you are not a superhero, and you cannot control automatic limbic responses (they are *automatic*). This is why it is so important to be gentle and compassionate with yourself as you learn these new tools. It is why you must allow each other mistakes and give each other "do-overs" and second chances and teach each other as gently and lovingly as possible about what you need in these moments. In the following pages you will learn tools for navigating emotional conversations.

Know When You Are Having an Emotional Conversation

In order to create a positive emotional feedback loop with your partner, you must first be able to identify when you have shifted from a regular, day-to-day exchange of information into an emotional conversation. Most of the time, people are not direct about the fact that they are having an emotional response to something that is happening in their life or relationship. They attempt to avoid the emotions by trying to "solve the problem" or distracting themselves from their feelings. However, your partner will probably indicate to you in some way that they are having a feeling. If they have had some practice in sharing feelings vulnerably, they may tell you directly that they are feeling hurt or sad. If they have not had much experience, they might tell you with indirect verbal cues, such as swearing or saying things in a lecturing or blaming way, or with nonverbal cues, such as a sarcastic tone of voice or an angry or sad facial expression. All of these are indicators that your partner is upset and that you have moved into an emotional conversation.

When we were teaching Bob and Courtney to identify an emotional conversation, Bob observed, "There are lots of times that I think Courtney might be feeling something, but I'm not always sure. I'm wondering if there is some way I can check." Together with Courtney, we came up with a sentence that felt neutral and non-blaming that Bob could use to check out his hunch with Courtney. If he suspected that they were moving into a feelings conversation, he would ask Courtney, "Are you having a feeling right now?" Courtney agreed that when Bob asked her this, she would take a moment to check in and see if her body felt shaky or anxious and to share with Bob if she was having a feeling and what that feeling was.

Remember, more often than not, if your partner is having a feeling, you will be feeling something too. You are a social animal, so your limbic system is aware of and sensitive to other limbic systems around you. This limbic connection with others is essential to your survival. When humans lived more primitive lives, if one person heard an alarming sound, their reaction would alert the other people around them, allowing the others to ready themselves to fight or flee from danger. When you spend a significant amount of time with a particular person, your limbic systems get more connected, so you will likely be more affected by the emotional swings of your partner.

If you start to feel a little shaky, your partner is probably feeling it as well. If they are triggered, you are likely to get somewhat triggered. Even if you are being "rational," your emotions are in the mix, and it is better to acknowledge this and move into an emotional conversation than to try to stay rational. Once you realize that you are in an emotional conversation, you can start the positive loop by harnessing the power of loving listening.

Harness the Power of Loving Listening

One of the most beautiful gifts you can give your partner is to *really* listen to them, especially when their feelings arise. In general, when people are listening to each other, they are only partially listening and a lot of their brainpower is focused on formulating a response, rather than on hearing what the other person is saying. When emotions are part of the sharing that needs to happen, the structure of and approach to your conversation need to shift to listening to your partner on a more limbic level. We call this loving listening, and it is one of the tools you will need to help soothe each other's fight, flight, or freeze responses.

As you've already learned, when people are being triggered and emotionally flooded, their limbic system takes over. It hijacks them away from a calm emotional state where they can use their relaxed feelings and thoughts to make good decisions for themselves. Telling someone to calm down or think logically is not going to help. When Kevin came to us, he didn't understand why his wife did not want to have sex with him, especially since she seemed to enjoy their sex together when they had it. As we worked with Kevin more, we found that he had a very difficult time dealing with his wife's emotions. Anytime she would cry or raise her voice, he would send her away, saying, "You're too emotional right now. Go calm down and come back and talk to me when you can be more rational." We shared with him that banishing his wife to have her emotions by herself likely made her feel lonely and disconnected. It seemed to her that he didn't want to deal with an important part of her, and she didn't want to share the rest. She shut down around her sexual connection because he was never available to be with her emotions. This is extraordinarily common in couples.

We taught Kevin how to listen to his wife's emotions instead of banishing her, and he was shocked at the results. "I never would have thought that just letting my wife cry and listening to her feelings would make her horny. Crying definitely doesn't make me feel horny; it makes me feel weak." Because men's emotions are repressed in our society, men don't generally feel the same amount of freedom and permission to release their emotions and move through them. They see their wife's or girlfriend's tears and think that if they themselves were crying like that, it would mean the world were ending. They don't understand women's ability to cry or that a woman might just need a "good cry." They have learned to suppress the urge to cry for fear of feeling weak or being ridiculed, though they would be much better off if it were more acceptable for them to cry as well. We often see men getting less support and attention from therapists because it is more difficult to detect when they are feeling something and they may not be good at detecting or reporting it themselves. For relationships of any kind to work, men need to feel and share their feelings and experience loving listening as well.

When you see your partner in pain, your first impulse is to stop the pain and fix the situation, especially if you feel like it's your fault. While there are many things you can fix in this world, emotions are not one of them. Your partner needs to be able to feel their emotions and let them flow through. When your partner feels safe and heard, they can offload whatever fear or threat is activating their limbic system, so that they can move back into a balanced emotional state. Your partner can do this only when they feel safe, soothed, and accepted. You won't always be the one who provides this safety – your partner will also need friends, therapists, buddies, support groups, or other resources. However, it is essential to intimacy that you sometimes be able to do this for your partner.

When one of you gets your feelings hurt in the relationship or there has been a breach of trust, you will likely experience some disconnection. Loving listening is the first step in the process of bridging this distance. Your ongoing ability to repair in the face of inevitable disconnection helps you and your partner create deep, trustworthy connection. Offering loving listening and trusting that your partner is capable of using adult tools to ask for what they need and make good decisions once they've been heard is the best way to support them.

When you are ready to listen, tell your partner that it is safe to talk to you. In order to create safety, remind your partner that you love them, that it is okay for them to feel whatever they are feeling, and that you are there and listening. When you are listening to emotions, there is not much else you need to do. You don't need to problem-solve, fix, or give a lot of input. The best thing to do is just join with them in their feelings. You can say, "You feel really sad," or "You were really hurt when I didn't respond to your email," or "You feel scared when I go on a trip."

When someone is triggered, they usually tighten up in their chest and face. They are holding the challenging feelings rather than showing them. A successful listening session is when you manage to support your partner in letting their guard down. Once they start sharing their feelings, they will often begin to cry or shake or sweat. These are good signs. You don't want to avoid these feelings; you want to help your partner let them out as much as possible. Trust in the process – when you listen well, your partner will be able to release their feelings and get their limbic system back to a calm state. Then they will be able to connect with you in a balanced way and will likely feel very appreciative of your having been there for them.

When your partner shows vulnerability by telling you they are sad or scared or angry, or by crying or shaking, it is a gift. It is a sign that they trust you enough to show you their most tender parts. Exposure of these tender parts creates deeper attachment and, sometimes, attraction. It is much easier to listen when it isn't about you, but it is especially powerful to listen when your partner is sharing a challenging feeling that was triggered by you. To help you listen when you feel that it might be your fault, remember that you didn't create the underlying feeling of insecurity or fear that your partner is having. It's more like you stepped on a land mine that was placed long ago, before you even met. When you step on this land mine, it might feel like it is all your fault, which makes you want to defend or fix instead of listening. If you can let go of self-blame, you will have a much easier time hearing your partner's feelings.

Listen with Embodied Empathy

Embodied empathy is the experience of feeling your partner's feelings and sensations with your own emotions and body. When you are connected to your own body and emotions and emotionally connected to your partner, you will often have a sense of what your partner is feeling. When your partner is upset with you, you will likely feel your own triggered feelings. In order to be able to generously listen and practice embodied empathy, it is helpful to follow a few simple (but not necessarily easy) steps.

First, remember that you are a good person who generally has the best of intentions. No matter what you do, you will sometimes step on your partner's land mines. If you have said or done something mean or hurtful on purpose, you probably felt threatened and very triggered yourself. No matter what, you will make mistakes in your relationship. This doesn't mean that you are not good for your partner or that you are a bad person. Be gentle on yourself. You may feel guilty, but continue to listen, so that your partner can have their feelings rather than caretaking your guilt.

Next, take some deep breaths and feel your own body. Notice where you feel tension or anxiety and acknowledge to yourself the ways in which you may be triggered. If you are too triggered, let your partner know that you are not capable of listening right now and see if they have the bandwidth to listen to you first. If neither of you can listen yet, see if you can breathe or take a walk together, or take a break with an agreement to come back together when you are ready to talk.

If you feel ready to listen, focus your attention on what your partner is saying and try to hear their feelings without preparing or rehearsing a response. Once you have heard what they have to say, see if you can put yourself in their shoes. It doesn't matter if what they are saying is "true"; the "truth" is their experience. Listening is a way to learn your partner's hurts, not a way to get the story straight. Empathy is imagining what it would be like for you to have the same emotional and physical response. Let yourself feel the other person's experience in your body. See if you can hear what your partner is saying using the wisdom you have just gathered with your embodied empathy.

For example, if your partner says angrily, "You expect me to read your mind and then get pissed at me when I don't do it the way you want me to, and I'm sick of it," you could follow the steps above and then respond, "That sucks. You feel like there are all these unspoken expectations that you are trying to meet, and when you don't meet them, I imagine you might feel like a failure."

Remember, you don't have to get the emotion right. Don't be attached to your evaluation. You are just offering some empathy so that you can create a dialogue about the way your partner feels.

Your partner's feelings in any given situation are likely to be very different from how you would feel in the same situation, because you have different fears and wounds. It is not helpful to say, "I feel the same way." Empathy isn't comparing or sharing how you would feel in the situation; it is understanding how your partner feels. They might say, "Actually, I don't feel like a failure. I just feel kind of set up and helpless." Then you just acknowledge the correction: "Okay, so it's more like you feel helpless, like there's this test and there's no way to get it right." Signs that your partner feels heard and empathized with include crying, a release of breath or tension in their body, softening their facial expression, nodding their head, or saying, "Yes, that's it," or something similar.

Acknowledging the parts that are about you without apologizing or trying to fix things right away is the final step. Your partner has experienced this feeling before their relationship with you and will continue to experience it. There may be ways that your wounds, and how you protect yourself when they arise, are interacting with theirs in a seemingly perpetual loop. Taking responsibility for your part in this dynamic can actually inspire empathy in your partner. For example, you might say, "I can understand why you might feel lied to. Sometimes I don't tell you what I need, because I often feel like I want too much. I try to ignore my needs and I don't ask for what I want, and then I feel disappointed that I don't get it." Taking responsibility for your part in the loop helps your partner trust you because they know that you are capable of self-reflection and sharing responsibility.

Know Your Communication Pitfalls

Once you know that you have emotions and a partner who may be willing to listen to them, the next step is to express yourself in a vulnerable way. When you and your partner try to talk about a challenging situation in your relationship, your hurt children may sometimes take over. While these hurt children have access to a mature body and vocabulary and may at first appear "adult," they communicate very poorly and with ineffective tools such as blaming, shaming, interrogating, threatening, or going to an incoherent place where all they can do is cry, scream, or freeze. In the most drastic cases, inner children can resort to violence and might even hit or hurt their partner in some physical way.

Let's compare some examples of the way a hurt inner child might share feelings with some examples of adult options that are more likely to elicit empathy in a partner. Often people learn ways of protecting themselves by example from adults (with active inner children) in their family of origin. Notice which of these approaches are your most common defenses and consider whether they were part of your family culture.

Blaming

One way that you may have learned to defend against your vulnerable underlying feelings and fears is by criticizing your partner's behaviors and blaming your partner for your pain. It is much easier to call attention to your partner's patterns and negative behaviors than to admit to your own or tell someone something that you perceive as a personal weakness.

Inner child: "Our sex life is falling apart because of you. All you care about is the kids. It's like I'm nothing to you."

Vulnerable adult: "Since the kids came along, I have felt unimportant and left out. I miss feeling desired."

Shaming

When you feel threatened by something your partner wants, you might use shame to try to stop your partner from having this desire.

Inner child: "Pornography is disgusting. I can't understand why you need to watch it. You're a sexist pig."

Vulnerable adult: "When I find out you've been watching porn, I feel threatened, like you really want to be with someone who is younger and thinner than me. I feel insecure and like I'm not enough."

Interrogating

You might demand answers to avoid feeling or admitting to your pain.

Inner child: "Why is it that all of sudden you don't do anything for me anymore? Do you even care about me? Do you even want to be in this relationship at all?"

Vulnerable adult: "I know you just got a new job and are really busy, but I so miss all the attention you used to give me, and sometimes the lack of attention makes me feel unloved."

Threatening

When you fear abandonment or you fear you might stay longer than you should in a harmful situation where you are unhappy, you might use threats in an attempt to get your partner to understand you and change.

Inner child: "If you keep talking to me that way, I'm going to have to find my own apartment, because I can't be around you anymore."

Vulnerable adult: "When you talk to me in that critical way, it makes me feel small and humiliated, and even though I really want to be with you, there is a part of me that just wants to run away."

Debating

Instead of dealing with the real issue (the underlying feelings, needs, and boundaries), you get hung up on specific facts and debate them. Debating makes the conversation much more tense and divisive, and the details rarely have any bearing on the real problem.

Inner child: "No, you didn't call me at 10:00 pm. It was at least 10:45 by the time you called."

Vulnerable adult: "When I think you are going to call me at one time and then that time passes, I start to feel panicky. The longer I wait, the more panicky I feel, and minutes start to seem like hours. It's that same old abandonment feeling and it really freaks me out."

Martyring

When you want someone to take care of you but you don't feel like you deserve it, you bury your needs or, when it feels safer to use guilt as a motivator, you martyr yourself so that you won't be rejected.

Inner child: "Oh, it's fine. I'll be fine. Please don't go out of your way—I'm sure I'll feel better soon."

Vulnerable adult: "I'm really hurting right now, but I'm scared to ask you for help because I'm afraid of being rejected."

Appeasing

If you learned that it was more important to take care of your parent than to acknowledge your own need or capacity, you might try to change yourself or take on more than you can handle rather than being honest about what you can and can't do.

Inner child: "I'm sorry that I didn't call you when I said I was going to. I'll never do it again.

Vulnerable adult: "I know that sometimes things I do hurt your feelings, and I care about you and want to be there for you, but I won't always do it perfectly."

Observing

Your inner child might have learned that it wouldn't be taken into consideration and assumes that no one will ever consider it or shift their behavior for it. Maybe you learned growing up that having a distant factual conversation is safer than telling someone how you feel about something, especially if you are certain that it won't change. However, if you let the other person know what you are feeling rather than stating a "fact," there is a chance that they might respond to your needs instead of defending their position against your observed "fact." At the very least, you will have done everything you can to garner empathy and advocate for your inner child out in the world.

Inner child: "It's just in your nature to be late. There's nothing to be done about it."

Vulnerable adult: "I know being on time is difficult for you and I completely understand. At the same time, when you show up late to events that are important to me, I feel hurt and unimportant."

Silence

Sometimes when you feel hurt, you want to punish your partner for not knowing what you need or feel. You want to teach your partner a lesson by giving them the silent treatment. Sometimes you go silent because it feels too scary to show such tender parts of yourself.

Inner child: " . . . . "

Vulnerable adult: "Sometimes I feel so hurt, I just want to punish you by not saying anything or by leaving you alone." Or "I'm too scared to share how I feel right now. It feels very tender."

Exercise: Identify Your Inner Child's Strategies

Take some time to write about your inner child's most common defensive communication strategy or strategies. When you are hurt, how does your inner child usually communicate? Are you a blamer? Do you get quiet? Do you try to win? Next time you are on a drive or a walk with your partner, share what you know about your inner child's strategies. Be sure to bring compassion and humor to the conversation!

Make sure each of you has a chance to share what you have learned about yourself and your inner child's defensive way of communicating so your partner can recognize it. Do not label your partner's ways; speak only for yourself. Taking a look at your own protective patterns and habits first instead of labeling your partner's is a very powerful tool for building intimacy. It is always easier to see and point out what someone else is doing; it is much more challenging, empowering, and transformational to reflect on and take responsibility for your own patterns.

Share Your Feelings from the Adult Place

When have enough awareness and self-soothing capabilities, you will be able to share your hurts with your partner in an adult way that makes them easiest to hear. It is never easy to share with your partner hurt or anger about them or to hear their upset about something you said or did. When each of you can share your feelings in a gentle, non-accusatory way, these messages are easier to hear and digest.

We have talked a lot about the importance of vulnerability to intimacy, but what does it mean to express something in a vulnerable way? Sharing feelings vulnerably means talking about yourself and how you feel, as opposed to expressing your opinion about how the other person is acting. Unfortunately, the former is much less common, because being vulnerable exposes tender, hurt feelings and you may feel afraid of your partner's ridicule, rejection, or misunderstanding if you share them. Many people think that being in an adult place means being calm and unemotional, but these are not the criteria for adult communication. In fact, if you are experiencing emotions but exhibiting none and acting "rational," you are actually using a childhood strategy. Being an adult means saying how you feel about what is happening instead of falling into communication pitfalls (blaming, shaming, etc.). You may cry or feel shaky when you are sharing, and that is wonderful. It means that your emotions are moving through instead of getting stuck.

Whenever you realize that a conversation or experience has hit on triggers, is important to realize that you are in an emotional conversation. Before we explain how to share your feelings from an adult place, it is essential to remember that, in an emotional conversation, you have to focus on sharing feelings and reconnecting before you move on to discuss logistics or make any decisions. Couples generally jump to decision making before they understand each other's underlying feelings, so they don't know how to properly take each other into account. Make a *foundational rule* that you do not have logistical or decision-making conversations until the two of you have reestablished your emotional connection. Most people can engage in reasonable discussions and make rational decisions once they feel their emotions have been heard, empathized with, and understood. No one is reasonable when they are a triggered child. Even if you make the "right" decision when you are triggered (in other words, the same decision you would have made if you had not been triggered), it will not feel fulfilling because you did it from a place of triggered disconnection instead of attachment, so it will be loaded with tension instead of arrived at from a place of teamwork.

Here's how to share your feelings from an adult place:

1. Check in with yourself and identify what you are feeling. There may be a mixture of feelings, tension, and reactivity. Take a breath. Check your Trigger Richter Scale and your Connect-O-Meter. Notice if you are feeling hurt, scared, angry, unloved, alone, etc. and see what is familiar about the feelings you are having. When in your life have you experienced this before, and how is it similar to feelings you had as a child?

2. Tell your partner what happened that upset you, and then tell them how it made you feel. "When you forget to pick up the kids, I feel like you don't care about me" *is not a feeling but an accusation.* Instead, say, "When you forget to pick up the kids, I feel responsible for everything, and that makes me feel alone and abandoned, like I felt as the oldest child having to take care of all of my siblings."

3. Give your partner time to empathetically listen to your feelings.

4. If it feels like your partner has understood and empathized with you, that's great. If it feels like they missed something important that you were trying to get across, clarify that part. Remember to give your partner the benefit of the doubt that they are doing their best to hear you. You may have to say something a few different ways or repeat it a few times in order for them to really get how it made you

feel. You're learning a new language, and it may feel clunky at first, so be patient with yourself and your partner.

5. Your bringing up feelings will probably trigger feelings in your partner as well. Ask them if they have any feelings they would like to share about what you just said. Use your empathetic listening skills to hear them. You may need to go back and forth a number of times, listening and sharing, in order to get through all of the feelings.

6. Once you feel understood, if there is anything you need from your partner in terms of soothing, ask your partner to give that to you. You can ask for a hug, a walk together, some time for a nice bath by yourself, words of reassurance, whatever you need to come fully back to your relaxed place. See if your partner needs any soothing as well.

Example Conversation: Bring Listening and Sharing Together

Sharon and Ashley came to see us after a huge fight about Sharon's drinking. Ashley was angry at Sharon for drinking when they went to parties together or out with friends. The night before, Sharon had come home after having beers with some friends, and Ashley had flown off the handle, saying, "You don't care about me at all. You come home drunk and you don't care about me. You're just like your fucking dad, and this is just another example. You only care about yourself and having a good time." Sharon responded defensively, "All you want to do is control me, and this is just another way you do it. I only had a couple of beers and suddenly I'm the devil, like I'm going to beat you or run out on you like my dad. You overreact to everything I do, and I'm sick and tired of it. I'm just trying to have some fun once in a while."

There are so many underlying feelings, fears, and needs in this conversation. In their session we helped Sharon and Ashley have a different conversation.

Sharon: When you came home last night and I smelled alcohol on your breath, I got really scared. I've asked you so many times to cut down on your drinking, and you promised me that you'd do it, so when you came home like this, I felt like I didn't matter to you. It made me feel mistrustful and I got really shaky.

Jackie: When I drink, especially after I've said I would cut down, you get scared and feel like you can't trust me. Is that right?

Sharon: Well, yes, and I felt very unimportant. It reminded me of all the times my mom promised me that she would come home early from work, or come to one of my performances, and then she'd just flake out.

Jackie: Okay, also unimportant. I can understand why you feel that way. I know you get really scared when I break my promises and you start to worry that it's going to happen all the time, or that you can't count on me. I think if I were you last night, I might have felt the same way.

Sharon: When you listen and understand me like this, I start to relax. It feels so much better than when you argue with what I'm trying to say.

Jackie: Is it okay if I tell you how it was for me last night?

Sharon: Yes, I'm ready.

Jackie: I want so badly to support you and help you feel safe in our relationship, especially after how much you were disappointed by your mom. At the same time, I want to be me and feel some freedom and acceptance from you. I did say that I would cut down on my drinking, and I was so careful last night. I had a glass of water between every drink, just like we talked about, and I only had three over four hours. When I come home and I see how angry you are, I feel like I can't do it right, and I want so badly for you to trust me and accept me for who I am. I like to have a drink once in a while because it relaxes me and makes me feel free, but I also want you to know how important you are to me. When I was a kid, it was always about my dad's rules. I couldn't put a glass down on the table the wrong way without him getting bent out of shape.

Sharon: I hear that you felt mistrusted by me last night and that you really want to keep me safe but also want to be able to have a few drinks and relax. I know I can be very sensitive when I think that you aren't keeping your promises. Even though you didn't say what time you were going to be home last night, I think part of me was wishing that you'd been home earlier. I know I need to tell you when I have these desires. The later it got, the more freaked out I got, and then, when I smelled the alcohol, that put me over the top.

Jackie: Oh babes, I didn't know you were missing me so much! I thought you had a ton to do and were happy to have me out for a while. You can text me next time and tell me how much you miss me. [Huge smile]

Sharon and Ashley are a perfect example of the way that attachment needs and individuation needs can interact and create big explosions, fears, or misunderstandings. Sharon needed reassurance of their attachment, and Ashley needed to know that she could still be herself in the relationship. At the same time, Ashley was happy to hear how attached Sharon was, because even though she needs freedom, she counts on their ongoing connection and needs attachment as well.

As they started to listen to each other and understand what was going on with their partner, we could visibly see the signs of reconnection. Pay attention to these as you work through challenging conversations. At the beginning, Sharon's eyes were hard and her body was tight. Ashley couldn't look at Sharon and was barely breathing. They were sitting far apart and were not touching each other. Once Sharon felt that Ashley was taking her feelings into consideration, she began to cry with relief and reached for Jackie's hand. Ashley was then able to look at Sharon and tell her what she needed. The more they understood each other, the deeper their breath got and the more they started smiling and flirting with each other again.

This conversation is an ideal one that happened with the help and support of a professional. When you try it at home, you will not do it perfectly. Neither will your partner—and neither do we!

Remember to give each other the benefit of the doubt that you are each doing your best and to look for the feelings and needs behind the words instead of picking on your partner about whether or not they are following the rules. The more you help each other in these moments the better!

Listen to the Hurt Child

In a perfect world, you would express yourself in a mature, adult way. Your partner would empathize, understand, and respond well to your feelings, needs, and boundaries. But you are only human, so it's time to let go of this ideal and realize that you won't always be able to express yourself in a perfect way. Your inner child is bound to emerge from time to time, and its ways of protecting you also keep you from intimacy. However, by listening to and caring for each other's inner children, you and your partner can give them the opportunity to have different experiences around their wounds.

Because your original hurts happened in the context of your early relationships with parents, peers, siblings, and caregivers, the most direct way to experience soothing and release around them is within a relationship. Your partner is your primary attachment figure, so your hopes and fears about relationships are directed at them. They are the person in the world who can trigger you the most. They are also the person who has the potential to offer you the most support and growth around your triggers. It is a profound experience for you and your partner to be able to trust each other and take turns caring for each other in the midst of your triggers. It is an opportunity to let your hurt inner child be held and cared for as it always longed to be. You can do this in a conscious way, where one of you maintains their adult awareness and capacities and holds the one who is immersed in their triggered, hurt inner child.

When your inner child is triggered, it will demonstrate the rigid behavior (withdrawal, aggression, spitefulness, etc.) that it developed in response to the hurt you experienced in childhood. Most people try to avoid these moments of triggering, but if you have vulnerably let your partner in, these moments are unavoidable. Instead, you can look at these as opportunities to deepen your trust and learn more about who your partner is and what they need. You cannot save your partner from their pain, but as one of the most important people in their life, you can offer them the experiences of loving support that they missed out on as a child. When your partner's inner child is running the show, they won't express their hurt in an elegant, controlled, adult way. They will express it in ways that push you away or make you defensive, so that it is challenging for you to listen and provide care.

When your partner retreats or attacks in a challenging way, try to see the hurt child underneath their adult words. Imagine a little boy or girl yelling, "I hate you, Mommy! I'm leaving." Obviously this child doesn't hate their mother. When they yell, "I hate you, Mommy," they really mean, "I need something from you, and I am not getting it, and that hurts." This is what your partner is trying to say. Because they are triggered, however, they are doing it like a child (albeit with the vocabulary and stature of an adult). As long as your partner is not being abusive and you are capable of holding their feelings from your adult place, listening to their challenging feelings can be an extremely rewarding and connective process. Please note that it is important to hold your partner's feelings, but you should not try to do so while you are being abused. Trying to do this will deteriorate your trust and attachment. Abusive behavior is non-consensual physical contact, violence, verbal threats or put-downs that attack your self-esteem, such as "You are stupid" or "You are useless and ugly," or emotional or financial blackmail. If your partner becomes abusive, or if the way they lash out is beyond your capacity to hold, we recommend that you state your boundaries and reach out for professional help.

Most people are afraid to offer support when their partner's hurt inner child emerges in a non-abusive way because they are afraid of reinforcing "childish" behavior. As a culture, we tend to condemn being childlike. But your inner child doesn't just disappear as you grow up, and there isn't an end date when you will be done with the triggers that your life experiences have created. Your inner child will stay with you your whole life. You will have a much stronger relationship if you accept that you need to get acquainted with and learn to positively interact with both your and your partner's inner child.

Research has shown that one positive indicator of attachment is when couples sometimes use a "baby voice" with each other. An intimate adult relationship gives people an opportunity to positively redo the attachment challenges that they experienced with their primary caregivers. Unfortunately, couples often end up repeating negative patterns rather than creating positive ones. If you can be loving and make room for each other's inner children while gaining tools to soothe your own and each other's limbic systems, you will develop a profound and sustainable connection. By loving and learning all about each other, you can actively become a soul mate to someone instead of imagining that you will passively find one out there.

When listening to your partner's hurt inner child, try to listen with love and warmth to the underlying need, not to the presentation of the need. If you continue to do this, the presentation should gradually become softer and softer. The idea is not to "work through" or "heal" or "fix" your partner's deepest fears, as many "healing" modalities suggest. Fears will arise in many different ways and sometimes in surprising contexts. Inner children and their adaptive strategies don't need healing—they need an adult to provide care and be a positive role model. Now that person is you. Your own and your partner's hurt inner children will be there for the rest of your life together, and if you progress with the model of listening, providing care, and being vulnerable, your inner child will become a relaxed, trusting observer rather than the part that's running the show.

When you hold your partner in the way they need to be held, they can soften around their hurt and feel more trust in you. Then, when the issue comes up again, you can repair and connect much more quickly and gently. The old wound will always be there, but there can be softening and more connective responses when your inner children are being held and heard. The best way to support each other while one of you has intense feelings and needs to release is to use a tool we developed while working with Macy and Adam. We call it listening to the hurt child; they lovingly called it "Tantrum Time."

Macy and Adam were a couple whose childhoods had required them to grow up before they were old enough to adequately handle the responsibilities of adulthood. Adam's dad died when he was seven, and Macy was the oldest of six siblings. Adam had to help care for his mom and take on more household responsibilities.

Macy was solely responsible for the care of the youngest three every day after school when her parents were at work. As we worked with them, we realized that they needed to introduce playfulness and their younger emotions into their relationship. We helped them develop a kind of game to play when emotions got really high in their relationship. They named the game "Tantrum Time" and used magnets on their refrigerator to track whose turn it was to tantrum next. Through a lot of trial and error, we discovered the ways that they wanted to tantrum and be soothed so that they didn't feel like they had to be grown-ups all the time and their inner children could get some care.

When either or both of them felt their fight-or-flight responses welling up, one of them would yell, "Tantrum time!" If they both needed it, they checked the magnets to see who would go first, but sometimes just one of them needed it. When it was Macy's turn to be the tantrumming child, she usually wanted Adam to hold her in his lap while she yelled and cried out all the things that were hurting. Adam would rock her and say simple things like "I know," "That is so yucky," "I'm here," and "Let it out." When it was Adam's turn, he usually liked to turn away from Macy, but she would sit close enough that he could hear her breathing and keep one hand on his back as much of the time as possible. He would yell or punch a pillow or just sit quietly and pout for as long as he needed to.

While they needed very different kinds of support, the support allowed each of them to be vulnerable, taken care of, and accepted for exactly who they were, even when they were feeling very young and hurt. Acceptance of every part of each other builds trust and is the glue that makes your relationship sustainable, strong, and fulfilling.

Excavate the Feelings

When you are listening to a problem that your partner brings to you, we want to help you listen for feelings, needs, and boundaries, regardless of how the message is being delivered. We call this excavating. It is like trying to find a rare gem buried deep in the dirt. Try to remember that negative approaches to communication are generally inner-child defenses. Despite the difficulties involved, you can listen to your partner with compassion even when they are falling into a communication pitfall.

If your partner is not able to communicate lovingly, you can do the translating for them as you listen. You do so by excavating— identifying or helping your partner identify the underlying emotions they are feeling and the needs they are having. If your partner says to you, "You're being such an asshole right now. Why don't you just leave me alone like you always do?" see if you can move beyond your defensive reaction and see their hurt inner child. Their tone conveys *anger*, and the words "leave me alone like you always do" might seem *lonely*, so you now have emotions to name and work with. You may feel *pushed away*, so now you've identified and named the hurt child's strategy. Thus you might respond by saying, "It seems like you're feeling *angry* and *alone* and that you want to *push me away*." Keep in mind that this hypothetical exchange is an ideal. Try not to hold yourself to perfection. It may be slow and awkward at first, and you may get some of it wrong, but you'll be surprised at how much the inner child is willing to help and redirect you if it simply feels paid attention to. Your partner might say, "No, I don't feel angry! I feel scared!" Then you could respond more accurately, "Oh, yes, you feel scared, maybe that I'm going to leave."

When Listening Isn't Balanced

Because everyone has different needs, boundaries, capacities, and wounds, relationships are not always fair. It is likely that one person will have more listening needs than the other. This can cause a problem if it gets too far out of balance. If one partner is always the loving, listening adult and the other is always the hurt child, it is likely that the partner in the adult role will build resentment, while the partner in the child role will feel disempowered and helpless. This parent/child dynamic can also create a unidirectional relationship, which can be disastrous for sex. Feeling like you always have to be a parent to someone will likely turn you off to having sex with them. In order to avoid resentment and the loss of sexual desire, it is important for the person who tends to be frequently triggered to do some individual work so that they can sometimes reciprocate by holding their partner's inner child. If you need a lot of holding, you can ask other people (such as close friends) if they would be willing to listen to you when you are upset, and you can find a therapist who can listen and also help you learn tools for self-soothing and self-care.

Enhance Your Connection

As you continue to get to know your partner through these reparative conversations, you will hopefully begin to understand each other's deeper wounds and the needs around them. Usually you can trace your triggers back to these wounds—wounds like "I am not enough," "People always leave," "I am too much," "There is something inherently wrong with me, so I can never be loved," "It is all up to me," "There is no one to rely on," etc. If you and your partner are able to identify these wounds, you can come up with special sentences to help each other during difficult times. Anish and Janice are a perfect example. Every time Janice would say, "I need to talk to you," Anish would be triggered, wondering what he had done wrong and expecting some kind of judgment or punishment. Janice would see Anish's anxiety and feel rejected because she was trying to reach out and share a difficulty with the hope of finding ways to repair and improve the relationship.

We offered her the special sentence "You didn't do anything wrong; I'm just having a feeling about something and I want to share it with you." When Janice tried this out in one of our sessions, Anish got a huge smile on his face and said, "Yes! If you say it that way, then I feel like I can just listen and that I'm not this terrible person who has screwed it up again." Janice also realized she was scared that Anish would grow tired of her complaining and leave, so she would hold off. When she finally said what she needed to say, she would be tense and angry that she'd waited so long. When she felt afraid, she asked Anish to say her special sentence. Anish would say, "I'm not going anywhere, and I want to hear how you feel." Hearing this brought tears to her eyes and inspired her to say what she needed in a calm way, without tension, fear, or blame.

Bring All Your Tools Together

In this first part of the book you have learned many tools to cultivate lasting love. You have connected with your inner child and learned to identify and express your needs, feelings, capacities, and boundaries. You have learned empathetic and compassionate tools for listening and communicating about challenging topics. You now look at your partner as someone on your team and give them the benefit of the doubt when misunderstandings and hurts happen. As often as possible, you vote for connection over protection and remember that relationships are about repair, not perfection. You take time to offer affection and appreciation and continue to see your partner as a growing, changing person who is beautifully unique. Finally, you support each other in cultivating each of your individual and shared dreams while continuing to build your trust and attachment.

In the next section we will discuss a topic that almost everyone tries to avoid: disappointment. We cannot stress enough that disappointment is a *normal* part of every healthy relationship. We will give you the tools to face disappointment head on, so that your relationship can thrive in the face of this inevitable challenge.

PART 2

DISAPPOINTMENT

D isappointment is normal. You and your partner are each unique, wonderful, loving people with your own sets of needs, desires, fears, feelings, expectations, and self-protective strategies. Sometimes you will meet each other's needs. Other times, in order to be true to who you are, or because of a lack of capacity, or because you are upset or triggered, you will not be able to fully meet each other's needs. This is completely normal, and it means that each of you will deal with some disappointment in your relationship.

Disappointment is such an important and unspoken part of relationships that we decided to devote an entire section of this book to it. Disappointment is frequent, inevitable, and normal, and it is important to directly address it in your relationship. Couples expend great effort in their relationships avoiding their own and each other's disappointments, losing precious time that could be put towards empathy and understanding. Avoiding disappointment causes you to hide parts of yourself, trying to be what you think your partner wants you to be rather than who you really are. In our experience, unprocessed disappointment inevitably leads to resentment and is the leading cause of separation.

In the relationships depicted in films and television shows, most drama is created by people trying to avoid disappointing their partner or trying to avoid their own disappointment. This avoidance leads to compelling drama: lying, cheating, discovery, and confrontation ensue. Eventually the characters confess what they feel. They share the intention behind their actions, and repair is made. This honesty about their original disappointments and how they were trying to deal with them is what creates the intimacy and connection they so desperately desire.

Why You Get Disappointed

Aside from the simple fact that no one is one hundred percent of what another person needs, there are three major reasons for disappointment in relationships. The first is that love is blind, the second is that life circumstances change and the final reason is that your needs and desires change throughout your lifetime.

Love Is Blind

We believe the statement "Love is blind" refers to that blissful ignorance most people have about their partner at the beginning of a relationship. During this honeymoon period, you tend to focus on what is working, how amazing the other person is, and how you fit perfectly together. This is a wonderful part of a relationship. It helps people get attached and fortifies them for the challenges they will face later. This blissful ignorance and the accompanying hormonal spikes are evolutionary necessities for creating relationships, bonding, and having babies.

During this phase of your relationship, you know very little about your partner. You might ignore information that doesn't jibe with what you want the person to be. You focus instead on what you want to see. If you do see something in your new partner that might be challenging for you, you might think that because you love each other so much, you can make your partner become what you want to them to be. You might omit some information about yourself because you feel ashamed of it or on the theory that because you will get to know each other over time, there is no reason to reveal everything right away. After the initial honeymoon period, however, you will begin to experience disappointment. Those little quirks that you thought were so cute in the beginning become annoying. You begin to see the parts of your partner that you successfully ignored or they successfully masked. Nathan and Haley are an excellent example of this.

Nathan and Haley began their relationship with a whirlwind honeymoon period. They both had the "love at first sight" feeling and decided to move in together after six weeks. At six months they gathered a small group of family and friends and got married at City Hall. Haley described their first year together as "blissful": "I felt like I was walking on a cloud. I couldn't believe that I had found a guy as sweet and caring as Nathan. For the first time I felt like I really mattered to someone. Before that, I felt like men just wanted me for sex, but Nathan really wanted to spend time with me and get to know me. What I didn't realize is that Nathan wasn't really interested in sex at all."

Nathan interrupted, clearly angry and upset at Haley's evaluation. "That's not true. I do want sex, just not the kind of sex that you want." Then Haley jumped in: "Well, maybe you should have told me before we got married that all you wanted to do was play with my feet." Nathan, clearly defeated now, responded, "I guess I didn't think you would marry me if you knew what I liked." As their story unfolded, we found out that Nathan had been too ashamed to tell Haley about his foot fetish. Instead he had used Cialis to have sex the few times they did so before getting married.

About a year and a half into their relationship, Nathan risked telling Haley the truth about his desires and his use of Cialis. Haley was understandably hurt by Nathan's omission. She felt tricked, and she was extremely disappointed because she thought Nathan's sexual desires were "weird" and she just wanted to have a "normal sex life." Nathan was disappointed as well. "I felt like Haley loved me so much, and she seemed to accept everything about me," he said. "I had never felt the level of acceptance that I felt with Haley and figured if anyone could accept all of me, it would be her. I felt so safe with her, I thought I could tell her about this and she would accept it too. Now she just looks at me like I'm some kind of freak."

In our work with Nathan and Haley, we helped them both see that people often approach the beginning of a relationship as a marketing venture. They try to show the other person all of the things about themselves that they think the other person will want, and they leave the other, more challenging parts of themselves out of the picture. As Haley later put it, "Yeah, I think I was being kind of fake in the beginning too. I mean, there were things that bugged me about Nathan, but he seemed to want my acceptance so badly that I just pretended I liked everything about him. I'm kind of a pleaser in that way. I'm really kind of judgmental, and I realized that I was going along with Nathan on everything and starting to get really annoyed."

We worked with Nathan and Haley to help them allow each other to be disappointed. Nathan was disappointed in Haley's judgmental attitude toward people she saw as different. When he shared this disappointment, Haley understood. She could empathize because she had felt something similar in dealing with her own dad. "Yeah, it really sucks to feel judged," she responded. Then she added, "Honestly, you ain't seen nothing. I can't repeat half of the words that came out of my dad's mouth about other people. I know I have some of that in me, but I try to be as open as I can."

Haley felt disappointed because she wanted badly to fit in with her friends, and when they had "girl talk" about sex, she felt embarrassed to talk about her sex life with Nathan. After Nathan was able to move past his defensiveness, he really understood Haley's fears. After all, he had spent his whole life fearing the judgment of others. "I get it, Haley. You just want to be part of the gang, and I really want that for you too! Honestly, you can decide what you want to tell them and what you don't. I just need acceptance from you."

Once they were able to accept each other's disappointment, we began to help them creatively explore a sex life that would work for both of them. It turned out that Haley loved sexy shoes and the idea of teasing and tempting Nathan until he could barely contain his desire. She would put on a pair of sexy shoes that Nathan bought her, strut around the house in them until he was shaking with desire, then finally let him touch and worship her feet.

Nathan felt so accepted by Haley that he wanted to be generous with her and give her her hottest sexual fantasy (what we refer to as a "movie") as well. He spent time learning how to give her pleasure and found that she was particularly aroused by the sensation of G-spot play, which he could do with his fingers. Nathan could get an erection when Haley let him touch her feet, but he still needed Cialis for intercourse, so if Haley wanted that, she would ask Nathan to take a pill before she put her shoes on. Each of them taught the other what they needed from sex. They found a way to incorporate both of their desires into their sex life and began to feel connected and grateful.

Life Circumstances Change

Changes in life circumstances, such as a new job or schedule, having children, or something as simple as a seasonal weather change, can sometimes create disappointments in your relationship. Let's take the example of Cal and Alena.

Cal and Alena met while working together at a telecommunications company. Alena was taking night classes to finish her bachelor's degree and working as a temp at Cal's company, where he was the director of marketing. They started dating during her temp assignment and courted while she was completing a teaching degree. They married after two years of dating and started trying to get pregnant. It took them three years, which were full of anxiety and stressful, fertility-focused sex. Alena had to take fertility drugs in order to finally conceive. After the baby was born, Alena suffered intense postpartum depression and Cal lost his job, two huge changes in their life circumstances that made their relationship much more challenging. Alena went back to teaching even though she hated it and Cal, in addition to taking on some freelance work from home, was the primary caregiver during their son's first year of life.

Before they got together, Cal had been competing as a pro tennis player and was ranked 150th in the world. Whenever Alena had the time, energy, and emotional bandwidth to watch the baby, Cal would meet up with an old tennis buddy and play a few matches. It was his one outlet for the stresses of his day. Being both a teacher and helping Cal with their son quickly became too much of a burden for Alena and Cal eventually stopped competing, losing one of his few social and emotional outlets.

Both Cal and Alena struggled deeply with their disappointment. Alena had met Cal at the height of his marketing career and loved the feeling of being able to depend on his financial support. Her childhood had been full of poverty and instability; her mother had lived in a mobile home, and Alena had been transferred from relative to relative based on who could afford to feed and clothe her at the moment. Throughout Cal's life, tennis had been his one constant resource. In the tennis community he found the support his own family had never given him. The exercise balanced his mood, and time away from his family refreshed him and made him more able to handle the ups and downs of daily life. Their drastic changes in life circumstances made their relationship much more stressful than it had been at first.

While Alena never directly expressed her disappointment, she started complaining about everything Cal did. She was frustrated and short with him and, when their fights got bad, she would pack some of her things, take their child, and drive away. Cal tried to stay calm during these fights and found other ways to escape his disappointment. He hid his tennis racquets in a neighbor's garage. Once or twice a week, he would dress up in a suit and pretend to go to a business meeting, lying to Alena so he could sneak away and play some tennis.

They came to us right after Alena discovered that Cal was playing tennis behind her back. She felt angry and betrayed, and Cal felt self-righteous and justified. They had experienced tons of pain and built a lot of resentment through this process. Although we tried to help them share and experience their disappointment and empathize with each other's struggles, the changes that they had faced caused too much tension and stress for each of them and they couldn't get back to a place of generosity and mutual support. When disappointment happens in relationships it is not always resolvable and we all soon realized that the process was shifting to divorce rather than marriage therapy. We did our best to help them minimize contact that could cause conflict and focus on amenable co-parenting.

People Grow and Change

In our work with couples we often hear one of them complain that the other "wasn't like that when we got together." This is usually said with anger and disappointment. When you fall in love, you feel attracted to and safe with the person you first met. You might make an ongoing commitment to them and move in or get married, imagining that they will continue to be the same person. At the same time, you might be excited by the thought of growing and changing together.

Sometimes the changes you and your partner go through are delightful; they add excitement and increased enjoyment or inspiration to your life. Other times your partner changes in a way that you find devastating or extremely disappointing. You may feel tricked or betrayed if your partner changes in ways that are surprising or confronting, especially if they are very different from what you signed up for at the beginning of the relationship. Parker and Anna's story is a perfect example of this.

Throughout her life, Anna had had difficulties with her physical health. She had aches and pains everywhere and discomfort with sex. When she met Parker, she was delighted because he was very understanding about her discomfort. He helped her in every way he could, and they had sex only when she was feeling most up to it.

After they'd been together for almost ten years, Anna's body had what she called a "complete breakdown." "I was so exhausted," she said. "Everything hurt. I couldn't even get out of bed. That's when I knew I needed to make a change." Anna quit her job as a corporate lawyer and went on a journey to learn about her body. She found out she had a number of food allergies and changed her diet completely. She also began practicing yoga and became a certified massage therapist. She felt in touch with her body but had almost no interest in sex.

Parker was disappointed that some of the things he most loved about being with Anna, like going out for a fancy dinner and a good bottle of wine, were now off the table. He was also going through his own changes. He began to admit to himself that his sexual desires were not limited to interest in Anna. He fantasized about group sensuality and sexuality and loved the idea of many people holding, loving, and touching one another and occasionally progressing to sex. He still felt very attracted to Anna and wanted her to join him on forays into group erotic experiences, but he no longer wanted to be monogamous.

When he brought this up, Anna was shocked. She barely had interest in having sex with Parker and had no desire to have sex with a bunch of people she hardly knew. She told Parker he was disgusting and needed to get some help, which is how they ended up in our office. In our work together we helped her see that no matter how much she shamed Parker, his desires were not going away. While he was staying true to his monogamous agreement with Anna, he felt very hurt and isolated by her judgmental attitude towards his desires.

As we delved deeper into their history, we found out that Anna's father had had multiple affairs and finally left her mother for a much younger woman. We helped Parker have empathy for her fears of being left and hurt as her mother was. Parker continued to reassure Anna that he loved their life together. He was awed by her growth and dedication to her body and her health, and more than anything else he wanted to share his life with her. He loved co-parenting, living together, supporting each of their aging parents, and sharing all the joys of life.

As Anna relaxed around Parker's love, she was able to let him dip his toe into experiences of group sexuality and connection. While she rarely accompanied him on these adventures and was never sexual with anyone else, each time he had an experience and came back to her with loving reassurance right afterwards, she felt safer and safer. He was very willing to go slowly and was happy to hold off on having sex with other people, but he wanted to attend sex parties and workshops and do some of the touching and connecting exercises those environments offered. There were and still are speed bumps and miscommunications, but Anna and Parker are each learning to experience their disappointment and accept the ways that the other has changed.

Journal opportunity: Disappointment
Write about some disappointments you have felt about your partner and some that you feel they have felt about you. Note which category they fall under.

The Ways People Deal with Disappointment

Disappointment can feel devastating; it can feel like you made a huge mistake and you will never get what you want in your relationship. While relationships offer you wonderful opportunities for growth, they are not there to meet every single one of your needs. This doesn't mean that your relationship is bad or that it has to end. When people feel disappointed that their relationship is not meeting some of their needs, they generally take one of seven courses of action. Some of these enhance intimacy and connection; others are more destructive.

Hiding Your Needs
The first thing you might do to avoid disappointment is to hide your needs. Unsure that your desires are going to be accepted, you go into hiding and don't share them. You may even hide them from

yourself or try to make them go away. There's a big problem with that: desires don't disappear. They build up or begin to leak out. They may build up and lead to depression or leak out in anger or through secrecy and deception. You might fantasize about leaving and not fully commit to the relationship. After all, why would you want to be somewhere where you can't be fully accepted? Perhaps worst of all, when you hold back on sharing your needs, you will build resentment. Resentment is the number one killer of relationships, so if you are trying to preserve the relationship by hiding your needs, you are working in the wrong direction.

Each couple's story above includes an example of someone hiding their needs. Nathan kept his sexual desire for feet from Haley until he finally felt that she might accept him, while Haley went along with everything Nathan wanted, ignoring her differing needs and getting frustrated. Cal hid his tennis playing to avoid upsetting Alena, and Alena hid her need for providership from Cal, leaving him in the dark as to why she was so angry. Parker tried to make his desire for group sensual and sexual experiences go away because he loved Anna and didn't want to lose her.

Pushing Your Partner to Change

Another way you might try to avoid disappointment is by pushing your partner to change. You might use tactics such as judgment, shame, guilt, or manipulation to try to get your partner to change. You might directly ask them to be different from how they are. We see one client, Orlanda, who feels like her husband, Ken, does not give her love in the way she wants it. She wants Ken to reach out to her constantly with love and affection, even if she is doing something that he doesn't like. He hates when she watches hours of television, but she wants him to cuddle up to her while she does it. She tells him, "You're so shut down. You don't know how to show love to me at all. If you were more open and initiating, we wouldn't have any of the problems we're having in our relationship." Whenever he tries to tell her what gets in the way of his showing affection, she tells him he is ruining the relationship. She has no room to hear his disappointment and, instead of sharing hers directly, pushes him to change. While they tried to avoid the disappointment for fear that it would lead to distance in the relationship, they ended up feeling distant and disconnected. Unless they do something to shift it, this cycle will continue to make them more and more distant from each other over time.

Staying and Building Resentment

You may have been in a relationship for a while and been faced with the challenges that come with having different needs, feelings, and capacities from your partner's. As a result of these differences, it is likely that you have built up resentments. Resentment is an indignant and stagnant approach to feeling as though you are being treated unfairly. You feel like the other person is hurting you on purpose and you do not to look at your own contribution to the problem. You may criticize but do not share your own or make room for your partner's vulnerability and you are not willing to share or hear your partner's needs. And again, resentment is the number one killer of relationships.

As a society, we look at longevity as the leading indicator of a relationship's success. However, there are many couples who stay together building up resentment and feeling dissatisfied, irritated, bitter or even disgusted with each other but not facing or working through their relationship challenges. These relationships can last a very long time, but we would not consider them successful because one or both partners are suffering and there is often very little real intimacy involved.

You may be in a relationship like this or have seen your parents or grandparents endure one for years. Usually couples in this kind of resentful relationship coexist in the same house constantly bickering or barely speaking to each other at all. They may sleep in different rooms and live very separate lives. They may also spend almost all of their time together out of habit but with very little enjoyment or pleasure. Usually these kinds of relationships are low on physical affection.

In order to unpack resentment and return to real intimacy, you may need to go through some very challenging feelings and memories. Many couples avoid this because it can be painful or bring up issues such as shame and fear. It can also be challenging because you may need to learn to empathize and accept aspects of your partner that you'd rather not face. We hope that, by using the tools in this book, you will find a healthier and more fulfilling way to relate to each other across your differences and disappointments.

Leaving

The divorce rate in the U.S. shows us that more than many people who enter into what they initially consider a lifetime commitment later end the relationship. For non-married people, the break-up rates are even higher. Clearly, most relationships don't last forever. Usually relationships end when the couple reaches an impasse that they feel they can't resolve in any other way. Many people hope that they will do better in their next relationship. However, people who get divorced and remarry are even more likely to get divorced again than folks in first marriages. Just finding a new person without transforming your patterns doesn't necessarily help. A successful and sustainable relationship comes from learning tools of self-awareness, communication, and empathy, as well as how to deal with disappointment.

We are not saying that you have to stay in a situation that doesn't feel right to you. What we are saying is that moving to the next partner won't help if you haven't learned how to do relationships differently. Better empathy, communication, and acceptance of your each other's desires and disappointments may not bring you and your partner to a satisfying place of connection. But at least you will have given your relationship every opportunity for success instead of just leaving and hoping to choose better next time. Without new tools, especially tools to deal with disappointment, the same or similar issues are bound to arise in your next relationship.

At the same time, you may have gone so long in pain and building resentment with a particular partner that the bond between you has actually broken irreparably. In this case, you may need to move on because there is not enough glue left in your relationship to keep you motivated to make it through the many challenging conversations and disappointments you will have to face. In this case it is time leave and the best thing you can do is to leave with as much kindness as possible reaching out for help in this process if you need it.

Staying and Sharing Your Disappointment

If you are like most folks in relationships, you are constantly trying to avoid or manage your own or your partner's disappointment without ever directly acknowledging or sharing it. Imagine your partner saying something like "I'm really disappointed that you often forget to call me and tell me that you are going to be late," and notice how you want to respond. Many people may respond by apologizing, getting angry or defensive, or promising to try to be better next time. It is very rare for a person to say, "I hear how disappointed you are. It must be really frustrating that I'm not good at calling you when I'm going to be out later than you thought."

There will be some behaviors that you can easily change to help your partner feel more comfortable and happy in your relationship. Others you won't be able to change or won't want to change. There are aspects of your personality, lifetime habits, or ways of being that you won't change even though they are hard for your partner to accept. In these instances, your partner will feel disappointment. We have found that allowing your partner to feel their disappointment while staying and listening to them lovingly is the best way to stay connected through these normal relationship challenges. It promotes trust, heals old wounds, deepens connection and intimacy, and fosters resilience and longevity of the relationship.

Chelsea and Angel had been together for six years when Angel lost her job. Two years later, when they came to see us, Chelsea was full of resentment; we could see it in the way she clenched her jaw when she described her frustration at their predicament. Every time Chelsea brought up Angel's job search, Angel would go into a long explanation about how she was in contact with a number of people about the job she wanted and was also looking into the possibility of doing her own start-up. While they had enough money to get by, when Chelsea suggested that they try to spend less, Angel would reassure her that it wasn't necessary because she was on the verge of getting a job.

In the middle of one of Angel's explanations, we stopped her and invited her to be with Chelsea in her disappointment instead of trying to fix the problem or reassure her that it would be fixed in the future. After all, it was possible Angel would get a job soon, but it was also possible she would not. "But I hate to disappoint Chelsea," Angel said. "I want to make her happy and I want her to trust that I can do what I said I would." We acknowledged how hard it was to just let Chelsea be disappointed but asked her to give it a try. After we gave her a few examples of how she could make room for Chelsea's disappointment, she said, "Chelsea, I don't have a job right now and I haven't for the last two years, and the truth is I can't guarantee when I am going to get one. I can see how difficult and disappointing that has been to you."

Chelsea started to cry as Angel finally made room for her years of disappointment. Chelsea said, "It's just been so hard, and I know you've been trying, but I felt like it wasn't ever okay for me to have any feelings about it. I've felt like it's all my responsibility to provide for us. It was so hard to carry this responsibility by myself. I felt so lonely that I couldn't share how hard and scary it's been, and you were so busy reassuring me that you'd have a job soon, you never even noticed how I've been feeling."

As the tension went out of Chelsea's body, Angel put a hand on her thigh and said, "I just felt you were so frustrated with me that you didn't even want to be close to me and that I had to prove that I could find a job before you would ever even want me again. I can see now how hard it was for you that I never even appreciated all that you were doing because I was so scared of your disappointment."

Not every problem in a relationship has an easy solution, but it is possible to help your partner release their resentment if you can make room for the disappointment they inevitably feel. To expand your skill set for listening and holding each other's disappointment, we recommend that you reread the section on listening earlier in the book.

While there are no statistics to tell you how much of your needs you can expect to have met in your relationship, we sometimes introduce the idea of the 70/30 rule. Since each person has their own personality, needs, feelings and capacities, fears, wounds and protective strategies, it is impossible to expect that anyone will be 100 percent of what we want all the time (no matter how many Hollywood movies try to tell us otherwise). It is possible that someone could be 70 percent if what we want. This leaves 30 percent disappointment. A relationship that tries to avoid all disappointment probably won't survive, as the couple's attempts to avoid disappointing each other will feed their resentment and drive them further and further apart. But love definitely can survive disappointment. It does so all the time.

Outsourcing

Some desires get met in your relationship, and some desires you outsource. Many times you outsource desires without even thinking about it; the outsourcing doesn't even show up on your or your partner's radar because you are both fine with it. For example, perhaps you love skiing but your partner hates it, so you have a group of friends with whom you go on weekend ski trips. Or maybe you like to talk a lot about your feelings, but your partner has a lower tolerance for feelings-based conversations, so you have a best friend you call when you are emotional and need some support. Problems arise when you have a desire that is not being met in the relationship but that you or your partner are not okay with you outsourcing. There is a big cultural taboo about outsourcing sex, but sex isn't the only thing that people feel uncomfortable outsourcing.

You might love partner dancing, and your partner doesn't want to do it with you but also doesn't like the idea of your doing it with someone else. Or you may not feel very supported by your partner emotionally, but they don't want you to share feelings with your friends, especially if you are talking about your relationship. You might be very extroverted and want to go out a few nights a week, and your partner only wants to go out once a month but gets very sad and frustrated when you go out without them. These are all examples of places where you could outsource, but doing so feels threatening or hurtful to your partner.

In your relationship, you are in an ongoing negotiation of desires, boundaries, and capacities. Each of you will need to honor the other's desires and be as honest as possible about your own, knowing that you will sometimes feel disappointment in the face of your differences.

In the following section we will talk about how people handle outsourcing in their relationships. Some people choose to outsource dishonestly, which can have many negative ramifications even if this outsourcing is never discovered. Others try to negotiate outsourcing honestly. While this might bring up fears, in the end, being open and honest about your needs brings the highest likelihood of long-term connection and personal fulfillment.

Journal opportunity: Outsourcing

Write a about the things in your relationship that you already outsource around. For example, "I do a lot of my emotional processing about my relationship with my friends instead of only with my partner" or "I go on hikes with my hiking group because my partner doesn't enjoy hiking and I love it."

Outsourcing Dishonestly

Outsourcing dishonestly means secretly doing something that you think your partner might not want you to do or something beyond what the two of you have agreed to. People do this all the time, and it is euphemistically referred to as "cheating," but we feel that is a misnomer. What you are actually doing is lying, and people lie because they are afraid, embarrassed, or perhaps excited by lying. You might be tempted to outsource dishonestly because you are afraid that your partner will no longer love, accept, or respect you if they discover certain aspects of you. For example, you might think your partner won't accept your desire for an occasional cigarette, so you smoke when you are out with other people and then make sure to wash your face and brush your teeth before interacting with your partner. Many people deny that they ever masturbate or watch porn, afraid that their partner will feel inadequate or judge them. You may feel excited by having a separate life or engage in taboo experiences without your partner's knowledge.

This might raise the question of why you wouldn't just stop smoking, masturbating, or watching porn. Some behaviors are harmful, and you actually want to stop but are having a very difficult time doing so. Other behaviors are essential to your sense of self and well-being. Smoking a cigarette or watching porn could be either of those. We want to differentiate between outsourcing dishonestly and having privacy. Privacy means that you don't need to tell your partner every time you smoke or masturbate, but they know generally that smoking or masturbating is something you do.

There are many problems with outsourcing dishonestly. The first is that it reinforces the belief that there are parts of yourself that are unacceptable and that you will never be loved for all of who you are. Second, even if your partner doesn't find out, it creates a distance between you. You start feeling like your partner is a cop or a jailer who doesn't allow you to be who you truly are. Also, lying and keeping up a lie takes a lot of mental and emotional energy. It keeps you hypervigilant and worried about being caught. Because your partner is connected to you, even if they don't know you are lying or what you are lying about, they may feel a disconnect. They may have a sense that something is wrong, or they may feel that they are going crazy because they feel something but don't know what it is. Finally, if a lie is discovered, it breaks the sense of trust, creates feelings of betrayal, and requires a lot of healing. Some relationships do not survive such a breach of trust.

Affairs

One of the most notorious examples of outsourcing dishonestly is affairs. In popular culture affairs are portrayed as the ultimate, unforgivable relationship sin. We think of affairs as more a symptom of problems rather than *the* problem.

Not everyone will have attractions to other people, but it is normal and common. It can actually enhance intimacy between you and your partner to talk about your attractions to others, what you feel about these attractions, and any insecurities or fears that hearing about each other's attractions might bring up. It is also okay to set boundaries around what you do and don't want to hear about your partner's attractions to others. When you make room in your relationship to honor the possibility of outside attractions and the feelings they create, it can help you stay connected and engaged with each other instead of developing separate lives where you keep your attractions hidden. This may help prevent affairs from happening.

People don't have affairs because they are bad people. They have them for many reasons. Sometimes people have affairs because they feel that something is lacking in their current relationship. They may still love and want to be with their partner (or they may not), but whatever is missing is something they feel they can't live without. Most people have affairs to make up for a lack of emotional or sexual connection. It may be that they don't feel accepted or desired by their partner, or they may desire sex that is different from the kind they can have in their relationship. Maybe the sex they are having in their relationship does not touch upon their core erotic theme, or there is little or no sex at all in the relationship. Some people simply have a strong desire for novelty and excitement despite a great sex life and connection with their partner; an affair can be a way to fight boredom and the frustrations that can arise when you are with one person for a long time.

Some people are comfortable with monogamy. Others feel much more themselves in non-monogamous situations. They may feel fully satisfied with their partner and still want to have sexual or emotional connections with other people. But because there is limited social acceptance of non-monogamy, these people usually feel that have no choice but to agree to monogamy if they want a long-term relationship. Some people don't realize that they want to be with more than one person until later in life, when they have already entered into a monogamous marriage. Eventually, their desire to be with someone else may win out and they may end up having an affair.

For some people, affairs are a way to escape the responsibilities and criticisms of daily life. They want to feel, for a moment, that there is nothing they have to do and that someone is crazy about them just as they are. Some people have revenge affairs to get back at a partner who has had an affair. Others have affairs to make up for a feeling of having been taken advantage of or as an expression of their unexpressed resentment. For example, if you feel pressure to provide and make everyone in your family happy, you may feel that the burden is unfair but not share your needs and feelings about it, instead making up for it by getting your emotional and/or sexual needs met somewhere else.

Avoiding Affairs

The best way to avoid an affair is to be honest about your desires up front, as soon as they arise or once you have overcome your sense of shame for having them. For this to work best, you and your partner must create an ethic of acceptance around each other's desires, even those that are scary or threatening. Some people are afraid to even share their sexual desires or talk about the possibility of being with someone else because they fear that their partner will judge them, stop loving them, resent them, or begin watching their every move to make sure that they are not seeing anyone else.

Another way to avoid affairs is to look at the boundaries you have set in your relationship or your resistance to certain sexual desires and practices. See if there has been any movement in those boundaries or if you are willing to explore the possibility of shifting them. Anna and Parker did a great job of this. When Anna first heard about Parker's desires for group sensual and sexual experiences, she was shocked and would not even entertain the idea of his pursuing these desires. But eventually she was open to the idea and even came along on some of Parker's adventures.

If you do decide to expand your boundaries, it is important to do so slowly and with lots of communication. It is also important to remember that trying something out to see if it is okay with you does not mean agreeing to it forever. There were times in Parker and Anna's relationship when Anna felt more comfortable with Parker's explorations and other times when she needed a break from them or needed to tighten the boundaries. For example, he attended a group workshop where he was able to give and receive erotic massage, and Anna felt great about it. Shortly afterward, however, she found out he was in contact with one of the participants and, while this was not outside their agreement, she got triggered, fearing that he might have an affair. Parker agreed to stop corresponding with the woman and took a six-month break from sensual and sexual experiences with other people in order to resolidify Anna's trust. Throughout, we emphasized to them how important it was that Anna not go beyond her boundaries and shift into resentment.

Another important way to avoid affairs is for each of you to make room for the other's disappointment when their needs are not being met. Often, if you are merely allowed to openly and shamelessly ask for what you want and receive the support of your partner in having those desires, that can be enough. Then, even if it is beyond your partner's capacity to allow you to meet those desires out in the world, they at least understand that you are disappointed, and you can feel loved and accepted by them.

You might also see if there is any part of your partner's desires that you can play with or explore through fantasy and role play. If your partner wants to have sex with other people, you might dress up, pretend you are someone else, and have them pick you up for a night of sex. You might have a secret affair with your partner, complete with afternoon rendezvous, or you might go out cruising together and check out whom you'd each like to pick up. If your partner desires threesomes or group sex, you might come up with a hot threesome or group-sex fantasy to whisper in their ear during sex.

For some people, just having their desires heard and accepted will be enough. Others might not be satisfied with this solution, and their partners will need to listen to their disappointment or discuss outsourcing. The longer desires go unspoken and unheard, the stronger they are when they come out, so early acceptance is important. For help beginning a discussion of outsourcing, see "Outsourcing Honestly," below.

Recovering from an Affair

Affairs can be extremely painful because your partner, in whom you've invested so much trust, has lied to you and broken an agreement. At the same time, if you want to recover from an affair, it will not help to think of one of you as the helpless victim and the other as the evil perpetrator. Once an affair has been discovered or confessed, you will both need to decide if you want to face the process of looking at the issues in the relationship (and the affair as a symptom of these issues) rather than labeling the person who had the affair the cause of the problem.

As noted above, we as a society think of having an affair as the ultimate, unforgivable sin. We rarely think the same of withholding love, sex, or affection, even though doing so can be just as damaging to your relationship. As the "injured party," the person who was cheated on may feel self-righteous and refuse to consider how their behavior may have contributed to the problem. They may refuse to have any compassion for the ways that their partner's denied desires or fears and wounds led to the affair.

At the same time, breaking an agreement with your partner creates a wound in the basic trust between you. Healing that trust requires that you listen to how your partner feels about the affair with empathy and without defensiveness. If you had the affair, you must make space for your partner to tell you exactly how they felt when they found out and how they are feeling now. If your partner had the affair, try to use your tools of vulnerability and share your feelings of hurt, rejection, anger, inadequacy, etc., as opposed to talking about how horrible your partner is. This will help them to be able to listen.

When an affair injures the trust between you, it will trigger your and your partner's childhood wounds. If you had the affair, you will likely need to listen to your partner's hurt feelings over and over again and keep reassuring them in order for them to heal and rebuild their trust in you. It can also be helpful to ask what kind of reassurance they need. For example, one person might need to hear "I'm not leaving you," while another person might need to hear "You are enough for me" or "You are the most important to me." Even the most deeply sincere apology isn't going to make the hurt go away, so don't jump to apologizing too soon. Give your partner the time they need to rebuild trust. It will also be important to eventually share with your partner why you felt you couldn't tell them about your desires.

Sometimes finding out about an affair and taking the time to talk and repair can be good for the relationship. It can be an opportunity to face the ways in which the relationship may have become stale or the reasons that one or both of you may have started hiding your feelings and needs from your partner. If you can move beyond blame and shame and talk about how hurt you are, you can move to a more honest, intimate, and real relationship than you had before.

To avoid future affairs, you will ultimately need to create a safe space where each person's desires can be shared openly. Instead of looking at your marriage or relationship contract as a fixed entity, you will need to accept that your needs and desires will change throughout your lives and that you will need to have an ongoing way to renegotiate if some agreement you have made isn't working. This way, you can feel safe and attached and be true to yourselves by celebrating your uniqueness and individuation.

Outsourcing Honestly (Non-monogamy, Polyamory, or Open Relationships)

Whenever we talk to anyone about non-monogamy, the first question we always get is "Yes, but do non-monogamous relationships *really* work?" The answer is that both monogamous and non-monogamous relationships have their places of ease and their challenges and they are quite different. For example, those who desire consistency and feel very threatened by the thought of their partner being with someone else may do better with monogamy while those who are more capable of dealing with jealousy and crave more variety may do better with non-monogamy. We believe the more important question is "What really makes a relationship work?" Whether a relationship is monogamous or non-monogamous, what makes it work is mutual trust, respect, attachment, good communication, empathy, the ability to self-reflect and grow, consideration, and the desire to support each other in being true to who you are.

There is no one-size-fits-all relationship model that works for everyone. The more you consciously co-create your relationship, the more likely it is to last. Currently, 51 percent of marriages end in divorce. Many couples who do stay together are very unhappy with their relationships, and others are outsourcing dishonestly by having affairs or seeing sex workers. Yet people generally do not ask, "Yes, but do monogamous relationships *really* work?" Monogamy is rarely scrutinized as a relationship model because, as a culture, we think of monogamy as "normal," "natural," or "right" and believe that staying monogamous with one person forever is the only truly successful relationship. The belief that a lifetime of monogamy is the only way sets people up for a lot of pain and failure, as even monogamous folks will generally have more than one partner in their lifetime.

We are not here to argue about whether or not monogamy is the way humans were meant to be. (For interesting discussions on monogamy and non-monogamy, check out *Sex at Dawn: How We Mate, Why We Stray, and What It Means for Modern Relationships*, by Christopher Ryan and Cacilda Jethá, as well as *Strange Bedfellows: The Surprising Connection Between Sex, Evolution and Monogamy*, by David P. Barash and Judith Eve Lipton.) We believe that different relationship structures work for different people. Some people will be more likely to sustain relationships if they are non-monogamous, while for others monogamy will be more sustainable. The most challenging relationships seem to be those in which one person desires monogamy while the other desires some form of open relationship.

It is essential to make a distinction between monogamy and commitment, since people often confuse these terms. You can be highly committed to your partner and not monogamous, and you can be completely monogamous without being committed. Commitment means being dedicated to working through the challenges that show up in every relationship. It means being aware of your own feelings, needs, and capacities and communicating instead of building resentment.

There are many reasons you might consider honest outsourcing as opposed to dishonesty or divorce. It can allow you to enjoy the depth of understanding and support that long-term loving connection offers and also experience the excitement of new partners.

Bringing in new people can often reignite passion between you and your partner. It can also make you feel accepted in all of your desires, which helps you feel more loving towards your partner. It can increase the stability of the relationship because no one needs to leave or lie in order to get their needs met. As one of our clients said, "He is totally there for me, is an amazing father, and also supports me in getting my sexual and emotional needs met. Why would I go anywhere else?!"

Negotiating non-monogamy can enhance your relationship because it requires a high level of communication skills that many relationships don't develop. We believe most relationships are under-communicated. Without a conscious choice to communicate, people get lazy about expressing their feelings, needs, and fears. Instead they use shortcuts and rely on what they already know about their partner. Imagining or practicing non-monogamy will likely uncover fears and insecurities that you may have buried and give you the opportunity to move through these feelings with the loving support of your partner. You can work through your fear of being left and insecurity about not being enough for your partner as you see them connecting with another person but still loving and staying with you.

There are also many challenges to non-monogamy. You may feel jealous or fear being abandoned, and you may feel hurt at times. Many people think they can avoid hurt in relationships, so they try to avoid any conversation that might bring up hurt or fear. However, any two people have differences, misunderstandings, and wounds that get triggered, and hurt is a normal part of relationships, both monogamous and non-monogamous. Offering good, loving listening will give you an opportunity to go through the hurt into a compassionate, peaceful emotional state.

If you decide to practice some kind of honest outsourcing, you will likely experience misunderstandings, imperfect communication, and crossed boundaries. Even if the two of you are very good at communicating your needs and boundaries around being with other people, miscommunication is still possible. Lisa and Andrei provide an excellent example of this.

Lisa and Andrei's open relationship developed slowly over the course of three years. They began by flirting with others and moved on to shared sexual experiences and occasional separate dates. Eventually, Lisa was ready for Andrei to have sex with another woman on a trip out of town. Before he left, she said, "It's fine if you go see her. I just don't want you to spend the night at her house." Later that evening Lisa called Andrei, who answered the phone and whispered, "Hold on, she's sleeping. Let me just step out of the room." Lisa's Trigger Richter Scale jumped to a seven. "What do you mean she's sleeping?!? I said you couldn't spend the night with her!" Andrei felt horrible. "I thought you said that you didn't want me to sleep at her house. I didn't know you didn't want her in my hotel room." Lisa responded, "Well, wake her up and send her home. I'm not prepared for a sleepover tonight." Andrei woke his lover up, explained the situation, and drove her home. Then he called Lisa back so that they could reconnect and talk about how the misunderstanding had happened. Andrei's willingness to keep Lisa's boundaries, listen to her fears, and work to repair the misunderstanding paved the way for potential sleepovers for both of them in the future.

If you want to explore opening your relationship with your partner, we strongly recommend you read some books on the topic. We recommend *The Ethical Slut*, by Dossie Easton, and *Opening Up*, by Tristan Taormino. We also offer five key pieces of advice:

1. Go slow. Start by doing something that feels within your comfort zone, then slowly move on to experiences that are only a little outside your comfort zone. We see the biggest problems arise when people approach opening up from a place of scarcity and urgency, feeling like they have to get everything from the first experience. Non-monogamy works much better when you take the time to test out new experiences and communicate afterwards to see what feelings arise and share what worked and what didn't.

2. Always prioritize your partner's needs and boundaries over the needs of other partners, and make sure your other partners know that you are going to do this. This may means you have to disappoint other partners in order to keep your primary relationship strong.

3. Do not expect your partner to have the same desires you do. When negotiating what you want, don't try to be "fair." Figure out what each of you wants to get out of the arrangement and whether you want to do it at all. For example, we worked with one couple where only one of the partners had other lovers and another couple where she wanted romantic dating with lots of kissing and occasional sex and he wanted anonymous sexual experiences with new people.

4. You won't know what it will feel like until you actually have the experience. Look at each new experience as a trial run where you see what you felt, whether it worked for you,

and what, if anything, would need to change in order for you to want to do it again. Some experiences will feel good, and you may want to do them again; others will not, and you might not want to do them again. If you stretched too far, you might need to try experiences closer to your comfort zone before you try to stretch that far again.

5. You and your partner will have different triggers around opening up your relationship, so it is essential to share your feelings. Don't ignore them or try to get over them without your partner's help. Don't compare your ability to handle an open relationship with your partner's ability. You each have your own feelings, needs, and boundaries. If you try to talk yourself out of any of these, you will build resentment and distance. To stay intimately connected, you will need to be as honest as possible about what is going on inside you.

In this section you learned that disappointment is an inherent part of a healthy relationship and that there are three major reasons for it (love is blind, circumstances inevitably change, and people grow and change). You also learned about the ways that people deal with disappointment: hiding their needs, trying to change their partner, building resentment, leaving, making space for the disappointment, and outsourcing. Finally, you learned why people outsource dishonestly, the reasons they have affaires, how to heal from affaires, the benefits of honest outsourcing, and how honest outsourcing can deepen your relationship, and you got some advice about how to open your relationship if you so choose.

In the next section we will dive deeply into one very important aspect of lasting, intimate partnerships: SEX. We believe sex deserves its own section because it is a topic so rife with misunderstanding and shame. As a culture, we are not educated or well versed in what it takes to have a long-term, fulfilling sexual connection. We want to offer you a full exploration of sex, what makes it hot and connected, and the role it plays in your relationship.

PART 3

SEX

As Esther Perel so aptly pointed out in her book *Mating in Captivity*, the forces that create hot sex are different from those that create great relationships. To have a great relationship, you need closeness, trust, and intimacy. However, passion is ignited by distance and uncertainty. The unknown of a new relationship might be scary and challenging, yet it also sparks desire and leaves plenty of room to project the fantasy of the perfect lover. While long-term relationships bring with them comfort, stability, and familiarity, they also bring about habituation and a loss of the excitement that comes from novelty and the unfamiliar.

It makes evolutionary sense that at the beginning of a relationship our bodies are flooded with the hormones that promote sexual desire. Research has shown that women's sexual desire becomes acyclical in the beginning of a relationship. Women generally experience peaks in their desire during ovulation and near menstruation. However, at the beginning of a relationship, the hormones that fuel female sexual desire remain steadily elevated, creating more opportunity for bonding and procreation. After this honeymoon period, they go back to their regular ebb and flow.

It is completely normal that sex and desire change in a long-term relationship. If you didn't fully take in that last sentence, we'll say it again: Sex changes in long-term relationships, and that is completely normal! If couples were taught to expect this, it would save them a lot of pain and confusion. As you move from the honeymoon period into the more lasting version of loving connection, it is highly likely that your sex life and/or your feelings about it will change in some way. Even if you are engaging in all the same behaviors you did at the beginning, they likely will not have the intensity and charge that were fueled by the uncertainty and hormones of the first year.

In order for sex to stay hot in a long-term relationship, it is important to cultivate experimentation, expansion, and growth. As a culture we are anorexic when it comes to sex: Our imagery and understanding of sex are very limited, underdeveloped, and narrow. In order to move from sexual anorexia to a five-course feast, you will need to open up to new ideas. You will need to face some of your shame or awkwardness around sex and engage in a learning process about your own and your partner's desires while taking it slow and being patient with yourself and your partner.

Most relationship books treat sex as something to be handled using the same approaches as emotional intimacy. Most books on sex offer a list of sexual techniques, with little understanding of the deeper need for psychological arousal. Better communication and empathy, combined with a list of new techniques, is not enough to reach your potential for pleasure as a couple. To explore what turns you on, you will need to see how your socialization and psychological development shaped your desires.

You must be willing to discover what really turns you on, even if it might be confusing or uncomfortable. You must be willing to learn with an open mind and a generous heart. In this section we will help you explore the playing field of sexual desires, from the basics of arousing touch to the fantasies that fulfill your deepest psychological needs.

To understand yourself and your partner as sexual beings, you must start by looking at the harmful social messages and myths that shape the way you think about sex. Then we can give you the tools you need to develop, enhance, and fuel your sexual connection so that it can last forever!

Move Beyond Damaging Myths

Before learning tools to enhance your sexual connection, you must first understand why sex can be such a challenging and contentious area in your relationship. There are so many confusing social messages and harmful myths about how sex is supposed to be and how men and women are supposed to behave sexually. Because these messages are presented to you from very early on, they become a part of you, like the air you breathe. Most people never question the validity of these messages and don't realize how harmful they can be. We invite you to question them and see how they cause misunderstanding, anger, fear, and sadness and how they disrupt your connection with your partner. Once you gain some freedom and distance from these messages, you can begin to approach sex with much more realistic attitudes and expectations, empathize with your partner, and better communicate your sexual needs and desires.

Damaging Myth #1: Sex is supposed to happen spontaneously

People often get upset at the idea that they might need to plan sex. They remember when they started dating and sex "just happened." However, dating is essentially planning sex or erotic connection. By planning a date, you are taking special time out to focus on the connection between the two of you. You dress up, fantasize about meeting each other, prepare, and get excited. This isn't spontaneous sex; it's anticipated sex.

Once you have joined your life with someone else's, time together has many purposes. You might spend time together where you are each doing your own separate work, or you might need to talk about money, kids, and all the day-to-day logistics of life. Most couples stop carving out time together where the focus is on building and enhancing sexual and emotional connection. When you live in a culture where there is a high level of shame surrounding sex, soon one or both of you will likely move sex to the bottom of your list of priorities. Just as you've made a commitment to each other, if you want your sex life to last, you need to make a commitment to consciously cultivate your sexual connection the same way you did when you were dating.

Damaging Myth #2: Sex is natural; you should just know how to do it

Most cultures approach sex with shame and repression. In families, sex generally is not discussed or is talked about with embarrassment and fear. In schools, sex education focuses on the mechanics of biological procreation, STIs, and pregnancy prevention; students are taught nothing about pleasure. Many religious institutions look at sex as sinful and preach abstinence until marriage. Yet after a childhood and adolescence in which you were taught to think of sex as sinful, dirty, and dangerous, you are supposed to fall in love and know exactly what to do sexually without ever having to talk with your partner about it.

In the animal world there is no sexual shame or repression. Bonobo monkeys solve most of their social problems with some form of pleasurable sexual stimulation. Sex is a natural part of day-to-day life, and primates learn how to have sex from watching their counterparts have sex. Because of our highly developed frontal cortex, desire is much more complex for humans than it is for animals. Our sexual desires are also shaped by our social environment. Monkeys don't need sexy lingerie, flowers, or blindfolds to get turned on. The idea that sex will just happen naturally between any two people, with all of their uniquely shaped sexual needs, is unrealistic.

You will need to learn what your partner wants instead of believing you should "just know." Even if you have been together for twenty years, if you have not talked openly about sex or taught your partner what you like, your sex life will likely be much less fulfilling than it could be. We once worked with a couple who had been together for forty years. When we started talking about sex and asked Courtney what she liked, she said, "One of my favorite things is having my toes sucked." Her husband's eyes widened. "We've been together for forty years. Why have you never told me that you like your toes sucked?" Courtney just shook her head and looked down. "I don't know. I guess I was just too embarrassed to ask."

Damaging Myth #3: Sex is supposed to be perfect

In the modern world we are constantly bombarded with images of perfect sex. Romantic movies, porn, and music videos are full of unrealistic, fantasy-fueled depictions of sex. Romantic movies show people wordlessly falling into sex and then flash forward to the same couple out of breath and happily fulfilled. In others, intercourse begins after a few passionate seconds and ends with the magical simultaneous orgasm during intercourse. In porn you mostly see contrived scenarios where the men have enormous cocks, the women are infinitely horny, and it's all sucking and fucking all the time. You rarely see what a fulfilling, realistic sexual experience might look like, and you hardly ever see those awkward sexual moments—when someone gets poked with an elbow or their body makes a funny sound. You almost never see people teaching their partners what kinds of touch, kisses, or words they want to receive. In reality, sex has its moments where things flow and its moments where you miss each other, moments of satisfaction and moments of frustration. Sex won't always be easy and usually isn't perfect.

Damaging Myth #4: If they loved me, they would know what I want

This is one of the most harmful romantic myths still actively circulating. While we discussed it earlier in the section on teaching people how to love you, we believe it bears repeating here. It is the unfounded belief that, if you have truly found "the one," they will know exactly what you want all the time without your having to tell them. While there are many wonderful people out there with whom you can have a great relationship, not one of them will know what you need all the time, or even enough of the time, without your having to ask.

As we said, your needs are different than your partners and they change throughout your life. You might think it is a good idea to show your sweetheart you love them by offering what to you feels like love instead of by asking what they want. You might also wait around patiently, then impatiently, then angrily and resentfully, wishing your partner would give you what you want without your having to ask.

To receive the kind of love you want and to give your partner the kind of love they want, you must kindly teach your partner how to love you and learn how to love them.

Damaging Myth #5: If I have to ask, it doesn't count

This is a close cousin of damaging myth #4: If they really loved you, you'd never have to ask for what you want. Many people believe that if you have to ask, it doesn't count. The truth is that it counts *twice*—once because your partner listened and once because they cared enough to try to give you what you wanted. We also often hear people say, "Well, I did ask, and they didn't do it" or "I asked, and they did it for a week and then stopped." Learning new habits takes time. This often means that not only do you have to ask for what you want many times, but you also have to allow your partner to practice, give gentle and loving feedback, and try again.

Heal from the Damaging Effects of Social Messages

So much misunderstanding and pain in sex and relationships can be understood by considering the different social messages that men and women get about sex and emotions. Because men are socialized and even rewarded for suppressing their emotions and women are repressed around their sexuality, men and women often end up with different needs around sex and intimacy. Women are told sex is dirty and not for them, so they often need a lot of love and respect to feel safe and comfortable enough to engage sexually. Men get much more permission for sex but are told they are sissies if they are perceived as too emotional. They put all of their emotional needs in the sex basket and feel most connected, accepted, and loved when they've been engaged sexually.

The most common power struggle we see in heterosexual relationships is "I need to feel loved to have sex" versus "I need to have sex to feel loved." Lesbian relationships involve two women socialized to say no to sex, which sometimes leads to less sex and more emotional connection. In gay male couples there are two men who were told they weren't supposed to feel, which can lead to a high sexual connection and lower emotional connection. It can be very helpful to look at your relationship through a social lens so you can see that the problems you are having are not personal but are shaped by your personal histories and society's rules about your behavior.

As you and your partner gain more perspective about the social messages you have each received, we hope that you will have more compassion for each other's needs and challenges.

Social Messages About Women

During their upbringing, girls receive very different messages about their sexuality than boys do; these messages affect their sexual choices and self-image as well as their ability to communicate about and feel entitled to pleasure. Because of this, women might rely on men's desire to help them feel their own arousal and desire. In fact, studies have shown that women don't feel sexual desire until they have actually begun engaging in sexual contact with their partner.

When it comes to sex, girls are simply taught to "just say no," while boys' "birds and bees" talks focus on a variety of topics, including "playing the field," wet dreams, and not getting girls pregnant. The talks that girls get focus almost exclusively on the perils of having sex. There is rarely any discussion of pleasure, and "playing the field" translates into highly negative epithets like being "easy" or a "slut."

Teachers and parents generally focus on teaching girls about reproduction, warn them about pregnancy, and tell them that guys "only want one thing." Girls are responsible for keeping boys' sexual desires at bay in order to maintain their virginity and avoid pregnancy. Socially, they get messages about the danger that sex poses to their reputation. Wanting sex, having sex, or liking sex means that they might be seen as a slut.

Girls who openly express their sexuality and enjoyment of sex and find themselves labeled "sluts" might react in one of two ways: they can deny their enjoyment or embrace it. Embracing it often results in being sought out by boys for sex but not for relationships and being ridiculed by both boys and other girls. Being shunned by the peer group is one of the most primal, devastating feelings a person can experience – humans, like other social animals, rely on the group quite literally for survival – and for girls, being shunned and excluded as a "slut" touches on this primal fear, so they avoid it at all costs.

Another heavily reinforced message in popular literature, movies, and television is that girls and women are valuable only if they are in a relationship with a man. To get a man, they have to be outwardly sexy and attractive but at the same time prove they are not "easy" by withholding sex until they have gotten some sign of love or commitment. Girls and women thus become the gatekeepers of sex. To fulfill this role, women have to shut down or distance themselves from their desires.

It is no surprise, then, that the most common sexual complaint among women is a lack of sexual desire. Ironically, girls and women are also supposed to dress and act provocatively, showing an external sexuality, while being disconnected from their internal desire. This can be very confusing to both women and men. As a woman, even if you do have a clear idea of what makes your body feel pleasure, it is likely that you rarely feel free to explain this to your partners. You may fear being too forward or aggressive about what you want, or you may fear you will be seen as slutty, easy, or unworthy of a relationship.

Women's sexual desire is also negatively impacted by all the focus on having a perfect body or looking just right. With so much pressure to look good, girls and women focus a tremendous amount of energy on being outwardly attractive as opposed to inwardly empowered. They are prized if they are beautiful (based on the culture's current standard of beauty) and criticized if they aren't, and in either case they receive demeaning or intrusive messages from the media, family, friends, and random strangers about their bodies.

With this kind of policing, there is no woman in the U.S. who does not have some negative feeling about some or all of her body. The women who appear to meet all of the cultural standards of beauty sometimes have the worst body image, as they are under more scrutiny. In a culture where women are valued for their beauty and desirability, one of women's deepest desires is to feel beautiful and sexy to their partner all the time – this allows them to relax into their bodies and feel sexual without worrying that they are being judged negatively.

In addition to being pressured to distance themselves from their sexual desire, girls are also told to be "good" and "nice" and to take care of others. They feel it is their duty to provide sex to their partner even if they are not enjoying it. They worry that asking their partner to do something differently might hurt their partner's feelings or be seen as unwomanly and jeopardize the relationship. The misleading cues, such as faked orgasms, that women sometimes give in order to make their partners feel good exacerbate the problem, since their partners don't learn that what they are doing isn't pleasurable.

Around emotions, girls are given much more permission than men to feel and express, while, at the same time being told that logic is better than emotions and that "women are crazy." These social messages create a situation where women often repress their emotions so as not to be seen as crazy and then explode when the emotions get to be too much. This cycle of repression and explosion makes them seem and feel crazy instead of them being able to just be comfortable sharing feelings, letting their emotions flow, and crying when they need to.

In the face of these social messages, women need to feel loved, accepted and desired. They need their emotions to be heard without being fixed and they need compassion and understanding if they are feeling sexually shut down. They need a place where they can express their desires to a partner who can hear and be responsive to them without defensiveness. They need a partner who loves and accepts their body and who gives them positive messages about their attractiveness and desirability. They need a partner who is willing to help them learn and grow around their sexuality while at the same time respecting their boundaries.

Social Messages About Men

Early on, boys received messages from parents, friends, teachers, television, and religious institutions about both men's and women's sexuality. Boys get the message that men are sexual and that their sexuality is a natural, animalistic drive. At the same time, boys sometimes receive the message that this drive is overpowering, wrong, and dangerous and that they must learn to temper and control it. In other situations boys are given the message that they should go out and exercise this drive as much as they want to, that they should "sow their wild oats" and put "another notch in their belt."

At the same time, both boys and the girls are told that girls are not really sexual beings. Boys are taught to believe that their sexual desire will not be welcomed or reciprocated. In boys maturation process, the combination of these two messages – that boys have an overpowering, animalistic sexuality and that girls are basically without a sexual drive – often leads boys and men to feel at least some level of discomfort with their sexuality. At worst, it causes them to lose touch with their own sexual power and confidence in their desires. Men who believe that women don't want sex feel like it is wrong to go after their desires. They hold back their erotic energy and try to be a "nice guy." Thus, men are supposed to want sex all the time, from anyone and are considered less than a man if they don't try to get it. While, at the same time, they are also told that women don't want sex, that they have to be polite and respectful and shut off their erotic power because it might be harmful to the women around them.

Men also receive the message that they must be ready for sex all the time, that they should have an erection whenever they are having sex, and that it should last as long as they or their partner wants it to. Because so much of male sexual prowess is focused on the penis, men's sexual confidence and pleasure are often tied to the size and ability of their cock instead of their overall enjoyment and ability as a lover. They feel responsible for providing sexual pleasure to their partner – and feel that they should be able to give their partner what she wants without any guidance. When men don't feel like a good lover, they may feel afraid of being judged or left, which can lead to performance anxiety and dysfunction.

In addition to the social messages about sex that men received, they also get very strong messages about repressing their emotions. These messages are enforced through social ostracization and physical violence. Boys who cry or act feminine in any way are often bullied or called misogynistic or homophobic names like "pussy" or "fag." Girls are generally given more permission for emotional expression and are comforted instead of teased when they are hurt or sad. The differences in socialization around emotions tend to lead to a great difference in the amount of emotion women and men allow themselves to feel and express, as well as the form that expression takes. Because men are taught to repress their emotions, they have less experience dealing with outward displays of emotion and are often overwhelmed in the face of a partner's tears or anger – particularly if they feel like they are responsible. Women are much less likely than men to separate emotions into "positive" and "negative"; women might talk about having a "good cry," which may sound to men like an oxymoron.

While women are objectified for their physical desirability, men are often objectified for their ability to provide. Women may look to men to provide financial security or emotional stability and support – or simply to fit into the boyfriend or husband role, because women are taught that their purpose is to be in a relationship. This can cause men to feel like they are not really wanted for their sexual desirability but more as an object of providership. Men may feel like it is their responsibility to save women when they are having challenging feelings and provide for them financially.

Ultimately, men have the same need to feel loved, accepted, and desired that women do. They want to feel like what they have to offer is desired by their partner, and they need to feel safe, even if they can't always perform in the way they need or in the way they wish they could. Men also want to know that their partner is aroused by what they are giving them sexually. In the emotional realm, men need a partner who can see that they are deeply feeling and sensitive people, even if they aren't always in touch with those feelings or able to show them outwardly. Men need their partners to know that they have feelings and fears. Additionally, they want a lover who cares about their pleasure potential and is willing to participate and play in ways that take them to their highest heights.

Understand the Challenges Created by Social Messages

These social messages and myths create an array of challenges in both women's and men's sexuality and inhibit people's ability to form satisfying and fulfilling sexual and emotional connections. As a result of these harmful myths and damaging social messages, many relationships end up full of misunderstanding, hurt, and resentment. Instead of seeing these differences and the problems they cause as a result of socialization, people often take them personally or judge their partner inadequate. These differences have negative outcomes for women, men, and couples, and they lead to low sexual desire and dysfunction for women, midlife crisis and dysfunction for men, sexless or low-sex relationships, and emotional disconnection.

Challenges for Women

Distractibility During Sex

Social messages cause women to be distanced from their sexuality and much more easily distracted from their sexual feelings than men are. They are worried about whether or not it is okay to have sex or are self-conscious about their bodies. Thus it becomes easy for little interruptions to cause women's arousal to drop suddenly. Intrusive thoughts about responsibilities can come in and ruin the mood as well.

Loss of Sexual Interest as a Mom

The image of a good mother is that she is pure, giving, and sexless. Women are supposed to live up to the social ideal of being a perfect caregiver, focused completely on her children. This image makes mothers feel like their needs are selfish, that sex or any other sensual, self-caring pursuits should be suppressed. We've heard so many women say that, when they became mothers, they didn't feel right doing all of the "naughty" sexual activities they once did. They stopped having many of the experiences that used to make them most aroused.

Low Sexual Desire

Many people try to figure out if women's lower desire is socially or biologically determined; we believe it is likely a bit of both. Because of hormonal differences, women have a somewhat lower sex drive; however, as we have explained, social messages also make it hard for women to connect to their sexual selves and cultivate their desire. Women have very high and usually unattained potential for pleasure: they generally experience more full-body sensation than men and can have varied and multiple orgasms. If your partnership has a woman in it, we want to help you move beyond the harmful social messages so that she can experience her full erotic potential.

Sexual Dysfunction

Since social messages are focused on scaring women away from sex, some women grow to fear sex and may experience psychological or physiological shutdown to sex. These shutdowns include vaginismus (painful spasms of the vaginal muscles leading up to or during intercourse) as well as anorgasmia (the inability to orgasm). Because of the negative messages around female sexuality, many women don't masturbate and never learn how to give themselves orgasms or how to teach their partner.

Challenges for Men

Midlife Crisis

Social messages are often what lead to men's midlife crisis. When we think of midlife crisis, what often comes to mind is a fortysomething man in a shiny red hot rod running off with some younger woman to find himself. Popular representations of this phenomenon paint this man as childish and selfish. The movie fantasy is generally that he wises up, realizes the error of his ways, repents, and returns to his wife and family. This popular depiction misses the point in many ways: it fails to address the underlying emotional, physiological, and societal reasons for this phenomenon. Men's bodies experience an abrupt and significant change in ability near age forty. As men are noticing their own physical decline, many are also seeing their fathers get old or die, which leads them to wonder whether they will get to live their lives the way they want to before they themselves die. The definitions of "good husband" and "good father" rarely leave space for men to continue doing the things they love to do in life without being deemed selfish and uncaring.

Sexual Dysfunction

Men may experience a psychological shutdown to sex because it feels terrible that their partner keeps rejecting their sexual advances. They don't want to push their sexual desires on their partner and are tired of feeling rejected so they stop getting erections. In addition, there is so much pressure on men to be sexual and ready for every sexual invitation that they aren't allowed the build-up they need to stay connected to their partner during sex. Instead they worry about their performance. Many men experience anxiety and performance issues such as erectile dysfunction, early ejaculation, and delayed ejaculation. In these cases we think sexual dysfunction is a response to a dysfunctional situation. If a man feels rejected or pushed to perform on command, his penis begins to rebel, as if to say, "I don't like this treatment" or "You can't make me do that." The fact that his penis is saying "no" to things that he doesn't want means it's time take a look at the situation and see if there is something that needs to change in the relationship not in him.

Challenges for Couples

Sexless Relationship/Marriage

Many couples come to us because they find themselves in sexless marriages. These marriages might be wonderful in every other way, with plenty of love, companionship, commitment, and cooperation, but one or both partners feel no sexual attraction or desire for the other. This can be a result of the different social messages they received. Sexless marriage can also be a result of partners having different desires (see "Hottest Sexual Movies" below) and not knowing how to communicate the differences. It may also simply be that one or both of them has lost attraction for the other.

As a result of social messages, women experience low desire and men feel inadequate and overwhelmed with sexual urges. This is not always the case, as a man can be very repressed around his sexuality and his partner more open due to an accepting sexual socialization. In general, however, the one who wants sex more will try to initiate and get rebuffed repeatedly. Eventually, that person will begin to feel rejected and undesirable, give up, and stop trying.

There is nothing inherently wrong with having a sexless marriage, provided that you are honest with each other and agree that it is what you want. If either or both of you want sex, then you may be able to learn how to reconnect with each other sexually. This section will help you find the energy, playfulness, and technique to meet each other's sexual needs. Alternatively, you may have to face your disappointment about your loss of desire and attraction and figure out how you will handle it. In that case, Part 2 of this book on disappointment will be helpful.

Emotional Distance
Men's and women's differing socialization can lead to a relationship that lacks intimacy, empathy, and connection. It is much easier to have empathy for someone when you can understand and relate to their feelings, fears, and desires. Because women's sexuality is repressed and men's emotionality is repressed, relationships can be full of emotional misunderstanding. In relationships, women often feel overly emotional or "too much," and men get labeled as emotionally unavailable. Because they are repressed and their expression is usually less overt, men's emotions can end up being left out.

Affairs
The emotional distance and sexless relationships that result from all of this misunderstanding often lead to affairs. One partner feels like some of their deep sexual or emotional needs are not being

fulfilled. Often they still love their partner and try to get those needs met elsewhere without breaking up their relationship or family.

One Couple's Plight Through the Lens of Social Messages

Mandy and Phillip came to us seven years into their marriage. Phillip dragged Mandy into the session because he wanted to have a better sexual connection with her. He shared that he had felt so much closer to Mandy when they had an active sex life, and he missed their connection. Mandy had not wanted to come because she thought sex was the only thing Phillip wanted from her. She also said that sex was not pleasurable and was sometimes painful for her. She felt like Phillip just wanted to use her and that he didn't care about her or their children. They both had very time-consuming careers, and Mandy felt that any spare time they had should be focused on their co-parenting. Phillip felt that they both gave a lot of time and energy to being parents, and he missed the wild woman he'd married.

They spoke of each other in very judgmental terms. Phillip described Mandy as "frigid," while Mandy said Phillip had a "one-track mind" and didn't care about anything but sex. Mandy did not want Phillip to touch her in any way, because she was suspicious that any time Phillip tried to physically connect with her it was only because he was trying to get sex. They spent the entire session blaming and shaming each other for how they'd ended up, which was so clearly shaped by the social messages they'd been given.

It took them three years to come back for a second session, and by then they were on the verge of divorce. Mandy had caught

Phillip cheating, and they were both overwrought. Phillip shared, "I tried everything to get Mandy to see that I was invested in our family and the children, but I just started to feel like I was dead inside, like there was nothing left that made me want to get out of bed anymore. I couldn't even get it up to masturbate." Mandy added, "I didn't realize how depressed Phillip was, but I can't believe he went outside the marriage and betrayed me like that! I still can't believe that sex is more important than anything else to him, even his family."

It took Mandy and Phillip months to begin to see how badly they had missed and misunderstood each other. Because Mandy had been taught that sex was dirty and unimportant, she didn't realize it was one of the main ways that Phillip felt accepted and emotionally connected to her. Phillip realized that he had been judging Mandy harshly, calling her frigid without realizing how she was struggling to be herself in the midst of the pressure to be a good girl, a good wife, and a good co-worker. As they started to see that they were both longing for deep connection as well as self-expression, they began to support each other and forgive each other for all the misperceptions and judgments. We were sorry to see that it had to get to this point of devastation before they were willing to really face each other's needs and feelings.

Journal opportunity: Social Messages
Write about the social messages that you have received about sex and relationships and how they have affected you and your partnership(s).

Sexual Rules to Live By

Now that you have seen some of the potential challenges you might face in your sexual and emotional connection, built a better understanding, and attained empathy for your partner, we want to give you some tools to begin to enhance your sex life. As you continue and expand your erotic adventure together, here are some very important rules to live by.

Rule #1: Don't judge

Most people are scared to share their desires and fantasies. After all, it's a big risk – few things are more private or make you feel more vulnerable. There are many judgments about what kind of sex is "good," "healthy," and "appropriate," yet almost all of us have some desires that lie outside those narrow bounds.

Your and your partner's desires are beautiful expressions of the deepest parts of who you are. Some of these desires will be realized in your life together and some will not. Some desires you will want to experience, while others you will want to keep in the realm of fantasy and may feel shameful about sharing. However, sharing them can create connection and intimacy between the two of you regardless of how much you are willing to guest-star in each other's "movies."

People often judge their partner's desires and fantasies because they don't want to be a part of them. You might feel obligated to fulfill your partner's desires or threatened by them because you can't or don't want to fulfill them. These fears may make you wish some of your partner's desires didn't exist. When sharing desires, it is essential to remember that desires do not necessarily have to happen – it is not your job to do anything you don't want to do. This brings us to the importance of boundaries.

Rule #2: You have a right to your boundaries

You and your partner both have a right to boundaries. As we discussed in the section on boundaries, it is essential that you keep your boundaries in sex to create trust and avoid building resentment. It is also important to remember that your boundaries may shift. A "no" right now doesn't shut the door forever. When you both feel permission to keep your boundaries, you will be able to relax and feel safer exploring. Each of you will also change and grow. What was a strong "no" at one point might become a "maybe" or a "yes" later. A "yes" might also turn into a "no."

If your sexual boundaries have been crossed in the past nonconsensually (for example, if you have experienced sexual abuse or rape), or if you have let them be crossed in your current relationship, you may need to keep your boundaries quite strong at first before you can let yourself trust again. Often when couples face boundary challenges, the person who needs strong boundaries feels guilty and the other feels rejected. As a result, the boundaries continue to get pushed and crossed over and over again. If this is your dynamic, you may need some support in learning how to negotiate boundaries so that you will be able to open up together in the future. Long-term boundary challenges can result in resentment, shutdown, and sexual dysfunction.

Rule #3: Try something new

No matter how long you have been together, if you have not approached your sex life consciously, with curiosity and open communication, there will be a learning curve. You can log many years of unsatisfying sex together without any improvement if you don't experiment. Trying something new can be scary, as it may bring up fears and inadequacies. But trying new things, exploring new ways of communicating around sex, and discussing needs and desires are essential to creating a good sex life.

Trying something new requires bravery and gentleness with yourself and your partner. Often when we invite couples to try something new, they feel awkward or goofy at first. When you first try a new experience, you might feel like laughing or making jokes. You might feel so uncomfortable that you want to give up. All of these feelings are normal. If you want to laugh, start out with something silly, like wrestling or tickling. If you feel like running away, play a game of hide-and-seek—one of you can run away and the other can chase after. You may need to cry or scream a little to release the tension. In other words, let yourself be free, silly, and real with each other in these explorations. Once you release some of the tension, you can begin to earnestly talk, look at, touch, and connect with each other in new and exciting ways.

Rule #4: Give each other the benefit of the doubt

Trust that each of you wants to please the other. If there is something you want from your partner and you have asked for it but they have not given it to you, there are some likely explanations. They may not know exactly how to give it to you, they may be afraid to try for fear of doing it wrong, or they may be trying to learn under stressful circumstances. If you are asking for what you need from a place of frustration or criticism, your partner may be triggered and their ability to learn shut off. For this reason, you must be patient and forgiving with your partner as they learn. While you might have a precise picture in your mind of how you want to be touched, seduced, and talked to, it can be challenging for your partner to know exactly what you mean. Feedback and repetition are essential to the learning process.

For example, when we teach men how to seduce women, we do an exercise called "Up Against the Wall." In this exercise we throw them up against the wall with passion and desire and then they take a turn throwing us. Whenever we teach this to men, we tell them that they won't do it perfectly on the first try. We always assume that they are doing their best and that, if they are not getting it right away, it's because they just need more *gentle* demonstrations, information, and feedback. They also need to practice, practice, practice.

On average, men will throw us against the wall about ten times in a session. Each time, we tell them everything they did that worked well for us and give them a couple of pieces of feedback about what could be better. We might say, "I loved it when you leaned in and smelled my neck; that was so perfect. When you come back out, make sure you come back into full eye contact before moving on to something else" or "Your big hands feel so good on my hips, and I'd love it if the grip around my waist were stronger." When you give your partner the benefit of the doubt, you will be more likely to approach them with a positive attitude and they will be more likely to learn what you need. If you've played sports or danced, you'll know that you don't learn complex athletic movements or dance routines on the first try, or even in the first week of practice. Sex is no different.

Rule #5: Trying it once doesn't mean you have to do it forever

In order to feel free while experimenting, it is essential to know that you always have a choice. You can try things out and see what is arousing and interesting for you and what isn't. Not every sexual activity or attitude is right for every person, and you will need to accept your own and your partner's interests *and* boundaries. If you ask for something and then realize that it doesn't feel as good as you imagined it, or only feels good when you're more aroused, feel free to say so. You can always change your mind. What works in your fantasy might not work in reality, and what works one time might not work for you forever.

Rule # 6: Ask for anything and everything you want

In order to get to the heights of your pleasure potential, you will need space in your relationship to ask for what you want. There are no right or wrong requests. When your partner asks what turns you on, you might think that the only appropriate answer is some sort of physical/touch technique, but that is just one of the many requests you can make. For many people, what turns them on has much more to do with psychological arousal than physiological, so just asking for how you want to be touched is not enough. For example, you might feel like it's okay to ask your partner for lighter touch but not okay to ask them to tell you what an amazing ass you have. We encourage you to ask for anything and everything you want.

For example, it is helpful to let your partner know what kinds of experiences get you in the mood to have sex in the first place, whether it be a walk in nature together, a sensual massage, a solo bath, a sexy dance party in the living room, dressing up and going out somewhere, getting sexts from your partner, or being thrown against the wall. Also, your partner may be thinking all sorts of wonderful, loving, and desirous thoughts about you but not know which ones will land well or how to say them best. If you help out by telling them, then they have a chance to do it right. The more specific you are, the more likely you are to get what you want. Try not to get frustrated when they don't get it right away or don't remember all the time.

Rule #7: Teach by showing

The ways you want to be touched, talked to, and looked at have to be taught through demonstration and practice. You will need to describe what you want, demonstrate it, and give gentle feedback. If you are teaching someone how you want to be talked to, then you will have to demonstrate the proper tone, inflection, and attitude. One of our clients, Dylan, was so frustrated and fed up with his partner's kissing that he had decided he just wouldn't kiss her anymore. Kissing was a central turn-on for his partner, Jacqueline, however, and she felt punished by his withholding.

In our session Dylan said, "I've tried to tell her a thousand times that I don't want her to just stick her tongue in my mouth right away." When we asked him why this was, he elaborated, "I just don't feel ready. I feel like that needs to come when I'm at a higher level of excitement, which might be just a minute away if she didn't start there and completely turn me off."

"Okay, Dylan, instead of explaining it, why don't you go ahead and give Jacqueline a kiss exactly the way that you want her to kiss back," we said, "and then, Jacqueline, you just follow Dylan's lead, waiting until he opens his mouth to open yours."

Dylan came towards Jacqueline with a closed mouth and began kissing, and Jacqueline immediately opened her mouth. Dylan became very angry. "See, it's like she's already way ahead of me!" he said, his voice full of frustration.

"Great," we said, "now we have a good idea of what's happening. Jacqueline, try keeping your mouth closed for the entire kiss and only opening if Dylan actually manages to get his tongue in between your lips."

Jacqueline smiled at the idea. She liked that there was a little bit of a game to it and that he was going to have to work to get inside. The next time Dylan leaned in, Jacqueline kept her lips together and he kissed her for a full two minutes and then just stopped. He had a huge smile on his face. "She didn't open her mouth at all. That was perfect. I could've done that for a lot longer but didn't want to bore you."

Jacqueline added, "I guess I knew what he didn't want me to do, but I never really got what he did want. I felt like I had stopped sticking my tongue in his mouth, but I'd never really done closed-mouth kissing before. I only had one boyfriend before Dylan, and if I didn't open my mouth quickly to match him, he would have licked my face off."

As you can see, showing pays off.

Rule #8: Accept your partner's desires without feeling you have to fulfill them

When your partner shares their desires with you, you might feel pressure to give them what they want. It is important to understand the difference between accepting each other's desires and having to fulfill them. If you feel like you have to fulfill their desires but you don't want to or feel like you can't, you may get scared and lash out with judgment, trying to prove that their desires are bad or wrong so you won't have to deal with them. It is scary to let some of your partner's desires remain unfulfilled. Yet if you try to do things for your partner that are not in alignment with who you are, your partner will be able to tell and will not really be getting what they want. Additionally, you will probably feel bad about yourself or begin to shut down and resent your partner.

Instead of giving your partner things you don't want to give, we suggest that you take two steps. The first is to hear and accept your partner's desire. The second is to see if the desire or some part of it is something that you feel comfortable fulfilling. For many people, having their desires heard and accepted is what makes them feel loved and connected. Others will want their desires to be met, but you might not be able to do that for them. If this is the case, and it is the case in many relationships, we recommend that you go back and reread the second section of this book, which discusses how to deal with disappointment in relationships.

Understand Your Sexual Brain

Understanding how your sexual desires are shaped and what you need to get out of sex is paramount to your sexual fulfillment. You or your partner may be surprised by what you find as you explore where your turn-ons come from and what you truly want. Ultimately, more than just to give and receive physical pleasure and orgasms, you both go to sex to *feel* something. These emotions might include feeling desired, taken, loved, connected, seen, punished, praised, ravished, competent, worthy, vulnerable, precious, powerful, etc.

As Jack Morin explains in his book, *The Erotic Mind*, your core sexual need comes from a conflict that you faced in your childhood that, through fantasy and sometimes masturbation, you were attempting to "solve." For example, if you didn't feel like your parents had much interest in being around you, your core sexual need could be that your partner be very passionate, desirous, and excited about you.

If it seemed like your siblings got all of the attention, you might get very excited about being "chosen." You might be attracted to someone who seems to be interested in many other people, so that you feel powerful because you can get them to choose you over and over again. If nothing you did was good enough for your parents, you might be most turned on by your ability to give someone else pleasure, because it makes you feel very capable.

Your socialization as a man or a woman also impacts your core desires. We find that since women were not allowed to connect with their sexuality, many long for a partner who will sweep them off their feet and take charge of the sexual experience. Because they are valued for their looks, they want to feel their partner's attraction and burning desire. Men want to feel like their sexual desire isn't overwhelming and they don't want to face rejection, so they fantasize about a partner who is overtly sexual and horny. As providers, they want partners who are turned on by what they have to offer sexually.

Exploring your and your partner's sexual brains is essential to understanding what feelings and experiences will be most arousing for each of you during sex. We call these core desires your Hottest Sexual Movie. In addition to biological desire, which will change throughout your lifetime, your sexual needs are what drive you to want sex. Your Hottest Sexual Movie is full of the fantasies and feelings you have during sex that are most likely to arouse you.

For example, watching anal porn or fantasizing about anal sex could mean very different things for different people. It may help you feel powerful/dominant or to feel submissive. It might give you the feeling of being let in to a very vulnerable place (you feel special) or of breaking a taboo (you feel naughty/dirty). Perhaps you've never done it before and it is a novelty (you feel free/exciting), or perhaps it is a few of these, all of these, or something else entirely.

It might be that you aren't aware of having any sexual fantasies. When asked about their Hottest Sexual Movie, women might hesitate because they discount many of their fantasies, as their desires might not be overtly sexual. Yet women have daydreams about how they want their relationships to look and what kinds of looks, words, acts, and gestures would fill their hearts and wet their pussies. Here's a Hottest Sexual Movie conversation we had with one of our clients:

"I never fantasize," Sophia said assuredly.

"Really? Have you ever thought about what your ideal date night might be?"

"Well, sure. My boyfriend Jorge and I used to go on these fun dates where he would pick me up, open the door for me, and whisk me off somewhere to eat and dance. Sometimes I imagine that we're going on these types of dates. We're both all dressed up and he brings me a bunch of stargazer lilies because he knows those are my favorite flowers. When he sees me, he tells me how gorgeous I am, and I see this look of love in his eyes."

Sophia told us that at the end of those dates, she could barely wait to get home and attack him, but she had never told him about her desires because she wasn't really counting this as a fantasy. Yet in this story we can see that Sophia got to feel special and loved. Jorge took the time to connect with her and buy her something that said he really knew her. Another of our female clients found that she got aroused when she was near running water and heard the sounds of nature around her. She wanted to feel that she was part of nature (sex is natural) and that it was okay to be in her body and have sensations. Unfortunately, she completely discounted this and defined herself as nonsexual because her wife's movie was about novelty and was much more overtly sexual.

By taking a broad-brush approach and looking at anything and everything that arouses you, you can identify what you want to feel and experience. Use the following exercise to make a list of one or more of the feelings that you want to get from sex.

Flesh Out Your Hottest Sexual Movie

Nearly everyone walks in the world with one or more sexual "movies"—images and ideas of how they want sex to look, what feelings they want to have, and what kind of experiences they want to live. The characters may change, but the themes generally stay the same. While most people have the ability to enjoy multiple forms of seduction, a person's primary sexual movie generally brings them the most pleasure and intensity. You can see many representations of women's sexual movies in romantic films. Many of men's themes are found in porn. There are also women who have more porn-like themes and men who have themes that are more often seen in romantic or passionate movies. More often than not, you will end up in a relationship with someone whose sexual movie is different from yours.

Let's pretend that your ideal sex is like a favorite movie. You like red movies, your partner likes blue movies, and every time you want to see a movie, you compromise and choose a purple one. The problem is, neither of you *really loves* purple movies, and you both come home every time not quite satisfied. Many couples' sex lives look like this. If you're really lucky, your lover has similar or complementary taste in movies, but while there is often some overlap, liking exactly the same movie is fairly rare. This can cause all sorts of hurt, misunderstanding, and frustration. Fortunately, if you communicate openly, support each other in these differences, and are willing to learn and "guest star" to some degree in each other's movies, you can create a sex life that is exciting, engaging, and fulfilling for both of you.

Solo Exercise: Identify Your Hottest Sexual Movie

Jack Morin suggests that the most efficient way to identify your "core erotic theme" or Hottest Sexual Movie is to take some time to write about your most arousing fantasies and most exciting sexual experiences. If you are exploring fantasy or porn, notice what you are thinking about right before you have an orgasm and pay attention to the underlying feeling or theme in that moment. Instead of focusing on the activities, pay attention to the feelings. Remember, many people will have dramatically different emotional experiences from the same imagery or experience. This exercise is to help you find out what you want to do and, more important, what you want to *feel* during sex.

Couple Exercise: Share Your Hottest Sexual Movie

When we work with couples, we always have a Hottest Sexual Movie conversation. These conversations have some very specific rules to follow if you want to make space for connection and intimacy. Before talking about the rules, we want to make an important distinction between Hottest Sexual Movies and fantasies.

Your Hottest Sexual Movie consists of the experiences you actually want to have. In addition to this, you may have a set of fantasies that you use to increase your arousal during sex or masturbation but that you don't actually want to fully enact in the world. For example, you might fantasize about group sex but have no interest in actually experiencing it. You might have more than one movie or might want to begin in one and move into another one.

Remember, when you are sharing your movies, it is essential to follow the Sexual Rules to Live By (p. 172), especially "Don't judge," "You have a right to your boundaries," and "Ask for anything and everything you want." Please review the Rules to Live By before having any kind of Hottest Sexual Movie conversation.

Create a safe space where you both can share this deepest part of yourself.

When you describe your movies, picture the character(s), the action, the setting, and what you feel. While it is a beautiful gift to really dive into the role of guest star in your partner's movie, you also have a right to decide which parts you are ready to try now, which parts you might want to add later, and which parts you may never do at all.

We encourage you to share both your movies and your fantasies as part of the conversation. When it comes to sharing past experiences with other lovers, be aware that this could trigger hurt. Be especially careful not to compare your partner to someone else with whom you've had amazing sex.

Know the Difference Between Psychological and Physiological Arousal

There are two main pathways to arousal: psychological and physiological. They are both essential to creating a hot, sexy, fulfilling experience, and putting them together is your winning combination. Psychological arousal comes from your Hottest Sexual Movie and the ideas and images that turn you on. Physiological arousal comes from direct stimulation of the body, the physical sensations of being touched. This can be anything from the light teasing of breath on your neck to the intensity of being grabbed forcefully, and what turns you on physiologically can vary greatly throughout your life and within a single sexual experience. As you become more aroused, for example, your pain threshold increases. You might like lighter touch at the beginning of a sexual experience but something more forceful later on.

There is also crossover between physiological and psychological arousal. Sometimes the way someone touches you physically has a connotation that turns you on mentally. For example, a spanking might feel physiologically arousing to your skin and also give you the psychologically arousing feeling of being punished. A gentle caress might give you goose bumps and also make you feel very loved and cared for. Conversely, psychological arousal may inspire your body to much higher levels of physiological arousal. For example, you might fantasize about an experience you had with a past lover that sends shivers down your spine and suddenly feel much more sensation from the stimulation you are getting on your clitoris or cock.

Learn What's on the Menu

In order to fully understand and share your movie, you need to be able to describe in detail what you want. There are five different aspects that you must cultivate: the story, the energy, the touch, the words, and the gestures. Because many people have no idea what their Hottest Sexual Movie is or how to describe it, we offer you an assortment of examples that we have heard in our practice, from the most common to the beautifully unique.

In each of the movies described below, we include some ideas about the story, the energy, the words, the touch, and the gestures that most often go along with that movie. You may find that your own movie is a mix of many of these examples. Choose from the following menu exactly what sounds most delicious for you.

Tell the Story

This is the narrative of the experience. For example, a romantic story will be about love, while passion is more about uncontrollable desires. A story is a narrative of what you might like to happen during an erotic experience. You don't need to have a perfectly coherent story with a beginning, a middle, and an end. It might be more like little snippets or ideas of experiences you want to have. For example, "I want us to take a romantic ride together up to a beautiful vista and just look at each other and flirt, building tension before we even kiss," could be the whole story. The more depth, details, and snippets you can offer, the more your partner will learn about what you want.

Exercise: Write Your Partner Five Sexy Texts
Write your partner five sexy texts telling them something you want that is related to your movie. For example: "When you come home, I want you to passionately kiss me as soon as you walk in the door, like you've been waiting the whole day to do it and can't help yourself" or "I want to take you out to dinner tonight; you can leave your panties at home."

Feel the Energy

The energy of a situation is the level of intensity. It can range from low to high and from out of control to highly controlled. Romance generally has a lower and somewhat controlled intensity, while dominance is generally a higher but still controlled intensity.

Passion has high intensity and is out of control. Getting in touch with your breath is foundational to connecting with yourself, your partner and your erotic energy. We cannot emphasize enough the importance of doing the breathing exercises below. No matter what kind of energy you are bringing, in order for the energy to move, you will need to *keep* breathing. If you want to maintain a level of intensity for a moment, like just before an orgasm or as you get that feather caress down your spine, you may chose to hold your breath briefly.

Exercise: Share Erotic Energy and Breath

In order to share erotic energy with your partner, you will first need to connect with your own body and the source of your erotic energy. The best way to do this is with Erotic Embodiment Breath.

Find a comfortable position sitting face to face with your partner, then close your eyes and begin to notice your breath. Breathe slowly, gently, and deeply in and out through your mouth. Breathing through your mouth encourages the breath more fully and deeply into your body. Allow your stomach, lower back, and pelvic floor to relax and make way for your breath to move more deeply down into your body.

Place your hand on the center of your chest and take ten slow, deep breaths directed into your chest. Do not force your breath but allow your chest to open as the breath flows towards your hand. Feel the breath rise and fall in your upper body and visualize yourself opening to sensations in this part of your body and to your emotional self.

Place your hand on your solar plexus (the upper part of your stomach right below your ribcage) and take ten slow, deep breaths into your stomach. Let go of being goal-oriented as you breathe into your solar plexus.

Place your hand on your pussy or cock and bring the breath all the way down to your pelvic floor. Take ten slow, deep breaths into your pelvic floor. As you breathe in, direct your attention toward your pelvic floor and imagine that this area is getting more relaxed. On the exhale, do nothing but simply let your body fully release the breath. By letting go of controlling your breath and muscles, you can feel your body open to eroticism.

On your next inhale, squeeze the muscles in your cock or pussy like you are stopping yourself from urinating, then exhale and release the breath. Take twenty slow, deep breaths with these squeezes.

On the last breath, inhale and hold your breath. *Do not let it out.* As you are holding your breath, squeeze the muscles in your cock or pussy, your pelvic floor, your fists, your chest, your legs, your feet your face, and hold, hold, hold. Then release the breath and feel the rush of energy move through your body. It can be very helpful to release with some sound, which invites the energy to shoot up through your whole body.

Take a moment to notice how you feel in your body. This breathing affects everyone differently. You may feel more present, relaxed, and aroused. When you first start doing it, you may also feel dizzy or tingly throughout your body. Sometimes this kind of breathing takes time to have its positive effects.

Now open your eyes and look at your partner while staying connected to your own energy on the inside. Let yourself share your connection, presence, and desire through your eyes. Begin breathing together and do another round of twenty breaths. Imagine that your breath and energy are moving between your body and your lover's. You can inhale and exhale at the same time or lean close together and inhale each other's breath so that you are breathing together in a circuit – one inhaling while the other exhales and vice versa. Play with different ways of sharing breath and energy.

Explore Touch
This includes the different qualities and types of touch that go along with each movie. For example, a light touch on the cheek is a timeless symbol of romance, while holding down someone's wrists during sex is a much more dominant touch. When touching, feel your hands as an extension of your energy and desire and feel them connected to your heart, stomach, and cock or pussy. Let the touch come from your core and touch for your own pleasure.

It may seem like the most generous way to give touch is to know what your partner wants and focus on giving them pleasure. But when you touch your partner, they want to feel your desire, and focusing entirely on their pleasure actually leaves you and your desire out of the interaction. In order for them to feel your authentic desire, you must touch them in a way that *you* enjoy. This is not to say that you won't need to learn anything about the way that your partner likes to be touched, but if you are focusing on technique instead of your own enjoyment, the touch will only go skin deep.

If you want your partner to feel the depth of your touch resonate throughout their body, you will need to touch for your own pleasure.

⟨⟩

Exercise: *Touch for Your Own Pleasure*
Start with the erotic breath above so that you feel a connection to your chest, stomach, and pelvic floor. Imagine that your hands are an extension of your cock or pussy and let your hands follow the desire generated in your body. Allow yourself to take pleasure in every aspect of your partner. Enjoy your partner's skin and squeezing their flesh. Delight in pulling them towards you and in their smell. Follow the internal voice of your desire as you explore all the ways you love to touch and connect with your partner.

Express with Words
Many couples have silent sex, where the focus is mostly on sexual acts. However, words help many people get their head in the game sexually. This is especially true for women, who are usually more distractible during sex. For some, however, words can be very distracting. Let your partner know if you like to hear or say things during sex.

Words can include direct statements about the other person, what you want to do to them, what you want them to do, or fantasies.

Exercise: Talk Sex

In each of the sections below on romantic, passionate, and dominant movies, we offer you a list of phrases that you can say to your partner. Take turns picking some of the phrases you want to hear from those lists or creating your own, and practice saying them back and forth to each other. If you need them said in a particular way, demonstrate to your partner the way that you want them said.

Show with Gestures

For some movies there are also gestures that you can make both during and outside of sex that can keep the feeling of the movie going, such as giving someone a heart-shaped chocolate or sending them a flirtatious text.

Go to the Movies

The most common movies that we see couples interested in are the romantic, passionate, and dominant/submissive movies, so we offer you in-depth explanations and examples of these movies. In addition, we include brief explanations and examples of the role-playing movie, the spiritual movie, the fetish movie, and the sensation movie so you will have a wide variety of movies to learn about and choose from. If some or all of your movie is not represented here, you may want to find a book, movie, or website that does a good job of representing your movie so you can more easily share it with your partner.

The Romantic Movie

The romantic movie is the most common movie in our culture. Most women were fed these movies starting from *Cinderella* and moving right on up to *The Notebook*. Almost all women respond in some way to romantic words or gestures. Even women who have passionate and/or dominant fantasies often want some kind of romance in the mix. Many men also have aspects of the romantic movie as part of their desires or sexual repertoire. While the romantic movies we see on the big screen almost never end in explicit sexual activity, we will show you what romance looks like in the bedroom.

The Romantic Story

The romantic movie is about being deeply loved and cared for—it's the soul mate fantasy. Romance is about holding each other as precious and uniquely, transcendently important. It is about the feeling that you know and understand each other deeply and pay attention to each other's wants. We had a client describe her romantic sexual movie so beautifully that it made us cry. Here it is as best we can remember:

"We both get dressed up – you're in some tight jeans that show the shape of your ass and that black coat I bought you, and I'm in an elegant dress. We go out to a restaurant together and you open and close the car door and the restaurant door for me. While we're at the restaurant, we touch each other across the table and you tell me how beautiful I look to you. When we leave, you put on my coat for me. At home you light some candles, turn on some of that music that has no lyrics, and invite me to dance. We start to sway together as you look into my eyes. You lean in and touch your lips to mine, barely kissing me, and then you whisper in my ear how much you love me. You move behind me and hold me close around the waist. Still dancing and swaying, I can feel your breath as you gently kiss my neck and ear.

"You unzip my dress and slowly take it off of me, caressing my body as it falls to the floor. You're surprised at my lacy white bra and underwear and you admire my body. You take my hand and gently lead me to the bedroom. We're standing next to the bed and you take one of my feet and put it on the edge of the bed frame so that my legs are spread. You tell me how beautiful my pussy is as you kneel down and begin to very lightly kiss and lick my pussy lips and tease my clit. You stay there for a while, just enjoying my body with no agenda, and then you pick me up and gently lay me down on the bed.

"You undress and lie next to me. We're facing each other, and you kiss my lips and caress the contours of my body. I feel so connected to you in every way, and I climb on top of you and put you inside me. We're looking deeply into each other's eyes, we tell each other, 'I love you,' and I start to cry because I feel you inside me in every way, our hearts and our bodies."

Romantic Energy

Romantic energy is what you feel in your heart when you experience the warm glow of love and connection. The energy that comes from the heart can be adoration or admiration. It is often what people are talking about when they refer to the feeling of falling in love. Romantic energy is both gentle and solid. You are giving and receiving the feeling of preciousness, and the energy moves between you like ripples of water moving across the surface of a pond.

Romantic Touch

The most romantic touch is light touch. Light touch is very arousing to the skin and body and therefore wonderful to use as warm-up touch, regardless of the movie you are playing out. The lightest and most arousing touch is called feather touch. It can be used on any part of the body to make it tingle.

To practice feather touch, use the whole palm while barely touching the skin. (Most people think that feather touch is done with only the fingertips, but using the palm or back of the hand can be more arousing because you get more coverage and connection.) Our bodies anticipate touch, so long strokes help move sensation everywhere. The strokes should be continuous so that touch feels smooth and flows through different parts of the body; if you take your hand off the body a lot, the touch can feel very disjointed. Make sure to vary the location of the touch, because feather touch can become annoying if it is repetitive.

While many people think of massage as a great prelude to sex, massage is relaxing as opposed to arousing touch. If your partner is very stressed out, it can be a romantic gesture to offer them a massage. This may invite your partner into their body. If you want the experience to lead to sex as opposed to sleep, once they are relaxed and present, you should move to lighter and more arousing feather touch.

Men's hands are generally larger and heavier than women's, and they may not have had a lot of practice with activities like combing another person's hair or stroking a baby's skin. It may be hard to imagine how lightly some women like to be touched. If you are a bit heavy-handed, try barely touching your partner's body at all, and have them tell you if they want it even lighter.

Touching romantically means taking a long time with gentle warm-up of the whole body. It includes focusing touch on areas of the body that are not overtly sexual, such as the face, hair, neck, or arms. Caressing the hips, back, waist, and thighs can also be very romantic.

Once you have used feather touch for a while, you will also want to bring in holding touch. Holding touch involves applying a firmer touch and keeping it there for a few breaths (at least three) without any movement. While feather touch arouses the body, holding grounds the body, encouraging arousal to spread through and sink deeper into the body. Holding also allows the body to let go and relax. It helps your partner trust your touch. You can hold your partner around the waist or back, or you can hold their hips, ass cheeks, or thighs.

Romantic Words

Romantic words have to do with beauty, preciousness, abstract sentimentality, fulfillment of dreams, and eternal connections.

Examples include:

Timeless attraction: "You are the most beautiful woman I've ever seen." "You are the man of my dreams."

Preciousness: "Being close to you means more to me than anything in the world."

The one and only: "No one has ever made me feel like this before." "I've never loved someone the way I love you."

Beyond the bounds of time or space: "I feel like I've known you forever, like we've always been together."

Physical appreciation: "Your skin is so soft/you are so soft." "You feel/smell so good." "You are so beautiful."

Using the "L word": "I love you so much, _____" (using your partner's name adds intimacy). "I love looking into your eyes/kissing your lips." "I love being with you."

Romantic Gestures

Because romance goes beyond the boundaries of the sexual experience, you can bring romance into your day-to-day life through both romantic words and romantic gestures. Romantic gestures include sending letters, cards, emails, or texts with romantic messages and giving gifts like flowers, a tie, chocolate, or a ring. Other romantic gestures are remembering special days like birthdays, anniversaries, first times (like the first day you kissed or the first time you met); dressing up to go out to a favorite restaurant, the theater, or dancing; or visiting a romantic place with beautiful views or stars. Romance is also experienced through deep eye contact, vulnerability, emotional sharing, writing an original poem or song, or sharing a poem or song that reminds you of your sweetheart.

Exercise: Talk Romance to Each Other

Create a romantic atmosphere by lighting candles and putting on some ambient music. Sit or lie down face to face and take a minute to silently look in each other's eyes. Breathe and allow yourself to notice how looking at your partner makes your body feel. Connect with your heart and your emotions, and take turns expressing how you feel about your partner using whatever words come to you while staying connected to your heart.

When you receive the words, take time to breathe and feel their effects on your body. There is no need to thank the other person for their words; allowing them to land will give the greatest satisfaction to your partner. If it feels awkward or funny at first, that's okay. Sometimes it is hard to take in deep feelings or compliments from your partner. Just keep practicing and breathing through the embarrassment. Take turns and enjoy yourself. This can be a great prelude to a romantic sexual encounter or an enjoyable experience in and of itself.

The Passionate Movie

The best word to describe passion is *animalistic*. It is sex that is a bit out of control. In this society we spend years socializing our children out of animal-like behavior. When the self-conscious part of your brain that tells you to be a good girl or boy shuts down, passion begins. Out comes the part of you that wants to bite, grab, growl, and satisfy all of your senses. In our sexually repressed culture, the passionate Hottest Sexual Movie is very common because it allows you to go beyond the constraints of being nice and compliant and makes you feel alive.

The Passionate Story

The passionate story is about intense, insatiable desire. It sometimes has the theme of a desire that you cannot seem to get enough of. Nothing captures the idea of the passionate story more than the passionate kiss, by now depicted in so many movies that it might appear cliché. However, when done right, it doesn't look or feel cliché at all. It is important to begin with a passionate look, letting all of the animalistic desire come into your eyes and holding it. Waiting before jumping into a kiss builds tension and lets you sit in the uncertainty of whether or not all the passion will be met. If you go too quickly to the kiss, you don't allow tension and excitement to build. By waiting, you allow yourself and your lover to build to a frenzy of desire where you can't rip each other's clothes off fast enough.

Here is a story one of our male clients told us about his girlfriend's passionate approach to sex:

"Usually my girlfriend seems to be more into romance, but every once in a while it's like she's possessed. It sometimes happens on vacation or when something really great happens in her life. I know it's happening because she gets this look in her eye like I'm just a piece of meat. I know women might not like feeling like a piece of meat and, to be honest, the first time I saw it I was a little surprised, but I definitely don't mind feeling like a piece of meat.

"This one time, she walked in the door wearing this really tight, sexy dress and she had that look in her eyes. Before she even got to me, she started taking her clothes off, and she just pushed me down on the bed. She started kissing me and grabbing me and taking my clothes off. She took my hands and started moving them all over her body, encouraging me to grab her ass and her nipples really hard. I could feel her grinding on me. Her pussy was so hot. I scooted up on the bed and she pulled her panties to the side and sat on my face, rubbing her pussy across my lips and tongue – I could barely keep up with her.

"She slid off me and pulled me on top of her, telling me to stick my tongue in her mouth and lick her lips and bite on her tits. I was completely engrossed. I mean, there was nothing else going on in the world except for her body, her mouth, and the smell of her pussy in my nose. My cock was so hard I felt like I was going to come as soon as I got inside of her, so I went slow at first. She grabbed my ass and encouraged me to press deeply inside. As I held still inside her, I could feel her clawing at my back, biting on my shoulders, and pressing her pussy onto my cock. I felt like she wanted me more than anything. I wouldn't mind being attacked like that any day of the week."

Passionate Energy

Passionate energy is about letting go of all of your inhibitions and allowing yourself to fully go after your desires. It is often a faster, more intense energy than romantic energy, and it is uncontrolled. As we talked about with the kiss, it is important to project your passion to your partner before you even touch them, giving them room to feel the excitement of the energy build. Make sure you give them room to move towards you as well.

Passionate Touch

Physical passion can include passionately and aggressively moving your partner's body around. Men sometimes fear their partners are delicate and easily broken, yet many men and women like to be touched, grabbed, bitten, scratched, thrown around, and ravaged. Fear that their partners are delicate can cause men and women to hold back their passion, especially if they feel that they have too much or that it will not be well received. Most women's bodies are strong enough to receive all the passion men have to give, and many women love to be picked up and moved into different positions. Passion might also include a lovemaking session where you make sure that you kiss, lick, bite, smell, or suck every inch of your partner's body.

The first time you bring the full force of your passion, your partner may be surprised. It takes confidence to stay with the feeling and not allow your partner's surprise or embarrassment to pull you both out of the experience. By staying connected to your desire, your breath, and your touch, you can invite your partner to meet you in this passionate place.

Intensify Touch

As the body becomes more aroused and excited, sensation thresholds change and you can bring in more intense touch. As arousal increases and endorphins flood the body, a more intense touch may serve to intensify pleasure. When you are adding more intense touch, make sure you intersperse light and feather touch. Consistently intense touch can cause the body to desensitize.

Grab asses and thighs. When it comes to approaching an ass cheek, you have to grab it like you mean it. Take a big handful, give it a good squeeze, and then hold on. Do not massage it or open and close your grip, and keep the following thought in mind: "Your ass is mine." This helps you avoid grabbing too tentatively or non-sexually and losing the opportunity for your partner's full response. Asses can take a nice strong grab, probably stronger than you think. Ask for feedback. This same kind of grabbing can be done on the inner thigh, although inner thighs can be more sensitive—don't squeeze them too hard.

Bite. Biting can be an extremely passionate and stimulating experience for both the biter and the bitten – an idea that vampire movies have exploited. Biting is an art that can bring extraordinary pleasure to the body, and it has been the cause of many fantastic goose bumps. For the greatest effect, biting should be combined with light kissing, breathing on the skin, and licking. The best places for biting are the trapezius muscles (located on the shoulder), other parts of the neck and shoulders, and the ass cheeks. Don't be afraid to bite hard – just make sure your hard bites are short and followed by lighter touch and kissing. Experiment and ask how hard you can bite your partner – you may be surprised.

Scratch. There is nothing like scratching to bring in the animalistic aspects of sex. Light scratching is a form of feather touch and can be very arousing at the beginning of a sexual experience. Your bodies may need time to warm up before they can get the most out of deeper scratching or gripping with your nails.

Combine Romantic and Passionate Touch

Combination touch is when you use one of the holding touches at the same time that you use a feather touch or an intense touch. Combination touch is powerful because the grounding of the holding touch allows the arousing stimulation of the other touch to spread and move more in the body. It also helps keep you both present with your sensations. This can be especially helpful if one of you is ticklish or easily distracted. All of the holding touches, including hair holding, waist holding, and ass holding, are fantastic when combined with light caresses on another part of the body, such as the back of the neck or the chest and stomach. You can also combine holding touch with intense touch, such as by holding the waist while pinching a nipple or grabbing an ass cheek.

Passionate Words and Gestures

Passion has to do with immediacy, intensity of desire, animalistic need, uncontrollable urges, and overwhelming feelings. Saying your partner's name passionately or commenting specifically on the aspects of your partner that drive you wild works well. When sharing your passion, you can use stronger, more overtly sexual language.

Examples include:

Tell them what you want to do to them: "I could eat you alive right now." "I could spend hours licking and tasting you."

Share the intensity of your physical need: "I can't wait to be inside you/have you inside me." "You make my cock so hard." "You make my pussy so wet."

Share how strongly you feel about them: "When you're near me, I feel like I'm going to explode."

Talk about how much they delight you: "When I feel you come, energy shoots through my whole body." "I love hearing you come/feeling you come." "I love fucking you/being fucked by you/being inside of you/having you inside of me." "You turn me on so fucking much."

Passionate Gestures
Passionate gestures include looking at each other with intense desire in your eyes as if you can't hold back any longer or breaking society's rules, such as by passionately making out in public or shouting out your window, "I'm with the sexiest man/woman in the world, and I want everyone to know it!"

Exercise: Throw Each Other Against the Wall
One of the most fun and enlightening experiences we practice in our coaching sessions is when we teach couples to approach each other with passionate intensity. One way we do this is to have them throw each other up against the wall. Before you begin this exercise, you might want to do a session of breathing together to get in the mood. During this breath-work session, you can explore a fantasy of what passion looks like to you.

1. Have your partner stand with their back against the wall. Stand about four feet in front of them and face each other.

2. When you feel ready, have your partner take a step towards you, as if they are greeting you or casually approaching you.
3. Look at them with all of your passionate intensity and push them back up against the wall, keeping eye contact. Take a break from eye contact to admire their lips, their muscles, or any part of their body you find sexy, but return to passionate eye contact periodically. You can also kiss passionately or lean in to smell your partner's neck. When you return to eye contact, keep enough room between your face and theirs that they can see you. Don't go directly to kissing, but instead hold the sexual tension of the look. This builds anticipation in the body, which is often lost in long-term relationships.
4. Even if your partner squirms, giggles, or doesn't know how to receive it, do not back down. Stay there with them in a relaxed state, looking in their eyes and staying connected with your passion and desire.
5. With one hand, hold them *tightly* around the waist.
6. With the other hand, caress their face, neck, and sides.
7. Play with variations of holding and caressing. For example, grab your sweetheart's ass tightly with one hand, lean in, and smell their neck. If you are tall enough, pin both arms above their head or behind their back with one hand and gently caress another part of their body with the other. Spread their legs apart with your knee and press your bodies closer together.
8. Take turns, with each of you doing this a few times and giving and receiving feedback about how it felt and what might make it even more amazing. Make sure you tell your partner what they are doing well and what you want them to do differently. You'll be surprised at how powerful this

exercise can be with additional information about what your partner wants and some practice.

The Dominant/Submissive Movie

Many people's core sexual need is about power in some way. If your movie is about power, you may want to feel like you have complete power or are powerless.

If you are submissive, you may want to feel restrained or contained in some way that makes you feel safe. You may want to feel like you don't have to take any responsibility, as if it is all just happening to you. You also may want to feel punished or coerced.

If you are dominant, you may want to feel powerful and in command. You may like the feeling of coercing your partner to do something and then having them realize they like it. You may want to be judgmental, scolding, or punishing.

You may find that at times you like to be dominant and at other times you like to be submissive. This is commonly referred to as being a "switch" and the act as "switching."

There are endless variations on dominant and submissive themes. Below we offer some ways you can play with dominant energy, words, and touch, and we invite you to bring your own creativity and flavor to any dominant/submissive play in which you choose to take part.

Dominance and submission can be a sensitive subject that requires finesse. Sometimes people who want to be dominated can be ambivalent about these desires, and whenever you are playing with power differences, it is important to be aware that this kind of play can provoke strong emotions. Not everyone is ready to play with dominance, and some need to feel a romantic or passionate connection before they are willing to explore it. Some people like light dominance but nothing heavy, and some *never* want to play this way.

Many women who believe in women's equality feel that they should not want to be submissive in the bedroom or that this power dynamic might end up leaking into other parts of their relationship. The truth is there are power differences in relationships, and dominance and submission can be one way to openly explore these differences. This is why we also recommend switching roles and seeing what it feels like for each of you to be on the other side of the equation.

There are also socialized and expected gender roles, making dominant women and submissive men less common in our society. Whether this is biological or social doesn't much matter; it is just a fact of the current playing field. This can cause challenges for some men and women, as they may feel ashamed of being in the minority or judgmental of their partner for falling outside gender norms. When two dominants or two submissives get together, it can be challenging. You might end up in power struggles, or with no one doing anything. This is why it is so important to bring a non-judgmental attitude to your Hottest Sexual Movie conversations. There is nothing either of you can do to change your partner's desires. You can, however, accept them without feeling responsible for fulfilling them.

When bringing dominance and submission into a sexual situation, you may worry that it is degrading to your partner and think that no one wants this. There is a difference between actually *being* mean and abusive and *playing* with dominance and submission. When a man or woman wants to submit, they do not feel abused; they feel taken care of and accepted. It might sound strange to think that spanking a woman or calling a man a "weak little imbecile" is taking care of them, but imagine your deepest, most exciting fantasy, and then imagine your partner offering that fantasy to you. Think of how cared for and accepted you would feel.

Many men mistrust the more intense side of their personality, and sometimes men fear that bringing out their dominant side will cause them to lose control. If you have a lot of unprocessed anger, it may be important for you to work on it with an experiential therapist. Through this work you will better understand and accept your anger, which will help you accept and trust all of the different aspects of your personality. Knowing you can stay in control is an important first step if you are going to engage in this kind of play. You can also begin with very light play and see what happens before going further.

Power play of any kind requires trust. If you are moving out of light dominance (such as an occasional spank or hair pull) into more advanced power play, you need to communicate about desires and boundaries. You also need a safe word. A safe word is a word that you would not normally use during a sexual experience that indicates that one partner is uncomfortable with what's going on and that the play needs to slow down or stop. Many people use words like "yellow" (to indicate slow down) and "red" (to indicate stop), while others choose their own unique word, which may have personal resonance or humor for them, such as "zucchini" or "mouse." The reason to use a word other than "stop" or "no" is that you may want to be able to use those words as part of the play to make it feel more realistic.

To understand what kind of dominant/submissive fantasy the two of you might want to play with, you may need to ask each other a lot of questions about what words and sentences you want to hear. This will help you know your role and how you want to play physically. It is also possible to bring role play into a dominant/submissive fantasy (see the explanation of role play later in this section) (p.222). If you are going to be doing rougher play like spanking, hair pulling, or flogging, it is important to talk about and practice with your pain threshold. You can use a scale of 1–10 to map your pain threshold and then tell your partner what number you prefer.

It is very rare to get the dominant/submissive movie right the first time. Both you and your partner need to be prepared to have a number of "takes" in order to find out what words and actions turn the two of you on the most. With regard to words, remember that tone and attitude are important, not just the words themselves. If your partner tells you something turns them on (for example, "I really like it when you tell me to get on my knees and then you grab my hair"), ask what turns them on about it. When you begin to get some insight into why particular actions are a turn-on, you can add others that are similar thematically.

They may say, for example, "I like it because I feel like you're in control of the experience and I have to do exactly what you say." On the other hand, they might say, "I like it because it feels like you're using me for your pleasure." These are two very different themes that would lead to different kinds of sexual experiences. The first could include pleasing you both, while the second would mean that, as the dominant, you would focus more on taking your own pleasure; if you focus too much on your partner's pleasure, they might get turned off.

Even if you've found some words, gestures, and experiences that turn you on, continue to communicate your needs and desires and give feedback. This will add variety and keep your explorations fresh and interesting. After all, there are only so many times your "professor" can give you a failing grade that you have to work to change, or your "house servant" can fail in their duties and need to be punished, before you may need to change the story and your roles.

The Dominant/Submissive Story

After a few sessions of learning each other's movies, a male client beamed as he told us this story about his wife:

"I had shared my erotic stories with her before, but I never actually thought to show her how to do what I wanted her to do. Now that we've had a few sessions practicing with you, I can't believe this is my wife. I mean, I knew she was bossy, so I guess I knew she had it in her, but last week I came home and as soon as I walked in the door she says to me in a stern voice, 'Take off your clothes, leave them by the door, and go to the bedroom.' I felt in trouble and aroused and immediately did as I was told. She left me in there for at least five minutes waiting naked, my anticipation rising with each moment.

"When she finally opened the door, she was wearing a tight, shiny black top, a short leather skirt, and boots I'd never seen before. She said, 'What are you waiting for? Get your ass on the bed and spread your legs and arms.' Patiently and methodically, she strapped me into the restraints you'd recommended. 'You've been a bad boy and it will be your job to lay there and please me until I'm done.' She had me watch as she played with her breasts and used a dildo and vibrator on herself.

"After she'd come a few times, she turned her attention to me, and I was so hard I couldn't stand it. She grazed my skin with the end of a belt and her hands and lightly slapped and spanked my thighs with the belt. She said, 'Now it's your turn to be my sex toy.' She alternated between straddling my cock and my face, either making me fuck her or lick her pussy.

"She turned around, leaving me a view of her ass and pussy as she slowly teased my cock with her fingertips and fingernails. 'I don't think I'm going to let you come right away, you dirty little boy,' she said, pulling my balls down hard and putting some oil on her hands, before continuing to stroke and tease me. Over and over, she teased me right to the point before orgasm and then she would back off and watch my tortured expression as I begged her to let me go over the edge. She said, 'I'll tell you when you can come. Your only job is to please me.' Honestly, I don't even remember the orgasm or if I came or not. It was just that feeling like she was in utter control of my body and was using it for her own pleasure that I think of over and over again. It never stops turning me on."

Here's another one told to us by a female submissive:

"I'm lying in bed half asleep when I hear him come into the bedroom. He shuts the door firmly behind him and locks it. He lies down behind me and with a very calm, slightly stern voice, he says, 'Don't move or speak; just nod if you understand. For the next hour you are going to do exactly what I say. If you step out of line or make a mistake, you will be punished. Do you understand?' I nod quickly. I'm already beginning to feel the heat between my legs and he hasn't even touched me yet.

"He rolls me onto my stomach and pulls my hips up so my ass is in the air. 'I like you in this position. I can see your pussy and you're at my mercy. Arch your back so your ass is tilted in the air.' I feel this sense of surrender inside of me; I want to please him and do exactly what he says. He doesn't think it's high enough. He says, 'Stick it up higher," and gives my right ass cheek a firm slap. I arch higher. 'Perfect.'

"He begins to play back and forth between lightly caressing my hips and ass and then pinching my nipples firmly. If I begin to relax too much, he slaps me on the ass to remind me to keep it high. He says, 'Spread your legs a little wider now so I can see you better.' He takes two fingers and puts them up to my mouth and says, 'Get them nice and wet so I can play with your pussy.' I begin to suck his fingers to get them fully wet.

"I'm up on my hands and knees now with my back arched towards his hand as he lightly strokes my pussy, then squeezes my pussy lips, then lightly strokes again. He takes my hair in his fist and moves my head towards his cock. 'If you're a good girl and suck it just right, you'll get a special treat.' I do my best to please him as he directs me, moving my head just the way he likes it. He tells me, 'Yes, that's good.' I suck it for a few more minutes and then he hands me a vibrator and says, 'Once I'm all the way inside you, you can put it on your clit,' he says. I get greedy and put in on my clit right away.

"He begins spanking me and pinching my nipples but I come before I surrender to his punishment. 'You're a naughty little slut, and now you are going to get fucked.' I am soaking wet by now and he shoves his cock inside of me. I'm working the vibrator and I can feel a lubed-up finger playing with my asshole as he is fucking me. Just as his finger begins to move inside my ass I come again, begging him not to stop."

Dominant Energy

Many people think dominant energy is angry energy. It is not. When you are dominant, there is nothing to be angry about; you are in control and your submissive will do what you say. If they get out of line, you can always punish them. So breathe deeply, relax, and figure out exactly what you want. And while you can be a mean dominant, you can also be a benevolent, loving dominant. The attitude of dominance can be a very centered and calm place from which to approach your partner. When you are dominant, you are in complete control. Take your time, go slow, be sometimes stern, sometimes gentle. Punish sometimes and reward other times. It is a calm but intense energy. The film *Secretary* shows an excellent example of a dominant/submissive relationship.

Submissive Energy

The energy of the submissive is that of surrender. You allow yourself to be taken over completely by the command of your dominant, receiving everything they have to give unless you reach your limit (in which case you will need to use your safe word). There are many ways to be a submissive or "bottom." You can be very good and obedient, doing everything your top says. You can also be an unruly bottom, feisty and fighting against their dominance but eventually being overcome.

Dominant Touch

While dominant touch can be intense, it doesn't have to be harsh or painful. Some dominance doesn't include any pain at all. If you want to add some intense touch to your play, we recommend combining it with gentle feather touch to create a broader, more varied experience.

When you are trying out new forms of dominant touch, remember that not everyone is going to like every kind of touch. This is especially true for dominant touch, where you are playing at emotional and sensational edges. Try different kinds and intensities and be very open to feedback.

Spank. Whether your sweetheart is "good" or "bad," if delivered correctly, an intermittent spank can be very erotic. There are entire workshops given about spanking alone, and there can be many wonderful nuances to a good spank. In the exercise below, we describe our two favorite spanks, which can be most easily incorporated into any sexual experience.

Pinch. For most people there are only a few places on the body that respond well to pinching. However, the response can be quite exciting, especially for people who like more intense touch on their nipples or ass. If your partner likes a lot of stimulation on their nipples, you can pinch while also pulling on or twisting them. Ask for feedback about pressure, twisting, and pulling intensity. Using ass or nipple pinching during oral sex might take your partner over the edge to orgasm.

Choke. Or, more accurately, hold the throat. The center of the throat should not receive any pressure. Instead, you can put light pressure on the sides of the neck. Do not cut off the flow of air or press the veins on the sides of the neck too hard.

Pull/hold hair. Hair holding or hair pulling can be a very irritating and painful experience if done incorrectly. We call it hair "holding" to contrast it with some of the rough hair pulling that is shown in porn. While some people might like their heads pulled back by the hair, for many this will be an uncomfortable position that may cause injury. Hair holding is quite different and can be very grounding and sensual. Bring your hand to the back of your partner's neck, spread your fingers, and comb your fingers up through the back of their hair close to their scalp. Then simply make a fist, keeping your hand close to the scalp. Be sure to make the fist slowly, hold for a minute or so, and then slowly release it. Never move into or leave hair holding quickly or you will lose all of the grounding and spreading sensations that it has to offer. Hair holding is great to combine with some other sensual or intense touch, such as kissing, biting, feather touch, or grabbing.

Tie 'em up. . . . with handcuffs, scarves, ropes, or a belt. You can tie arms or legs or both; just make sure you tie them in such a way that you can reach your favorite parts and check to make sure blood is circulating to hands and feet throughout the play. If the tied-up person feels any tingling sensation, take a break and loosen the ties. If you are not into the process of tying someone, there are some great toys that use Velcro, making quick restraint possible.

Blindfold. You can buy blindfolds made of leather or soft, silky material or use a shirt or scarf in the heat of the moment. Blindfolding takes away your partner's ability to know what's coming next, so that you can bring in elements of surprise. When you are blindfolded, your sense of sight is gone, allowing you to focus on the heightened pleasure of your other senses.

Spit. Spitting on your submissive partner or into their mouth can add a feeling of degradation or punishment if your submissive needs that. It can also become a way to reward your partner for being good by allowing them to drink a part of you.

Dominant Words

Dominant words can create a host of feelings in your submissive. Using these words will show that you are in command and have confidence and power. From this place you can give and take away permission or offer praise or punishment. You might use words to make your submissive feel degraded or possessed. Deliver words with a calm, commanding tone, and do not ask— *tell* your partner what to do. Saying, "Please turn around and get on your knees," is very different from saying, "Get on your knees and stick your ass in the air." When in the dominant position, use commands and avoid prefacing these commands with "I want you to" or "Will you." Of course they will; they are at your mercy. If they won't, you can always punish them and, if it goes too far, they have their safe word to slow you down or stop you. If they do what you say, you can reward them with something that they want sexually or grant them the gift of accessing your body and pleasuring you.

Command:

"Spread your legs and show me your pussy."
"Get on your knees and lick my boot."
"Open your mouth."
"Stick your ass in the air."

Revoke permission:

"Did I tell you it was okay to look at me? Look at the ground."

Praise:

"You've been a very good girl/boy. Come here and I'll stroke your hair."

Punish/degrade:

"You're a dirty (naughty, nasty) little slut."
"You're a little sissy."

Disapprove:

"I told you to stick your tongue in me. Is that as far as you can go?"

"You're going to need to try a lot harder than that."
"You call that masturbating? Stick your fingers inside yourself."

Possess:

"That's my cock/pussy. I'll tell you when you can touch it."
"That's my ass. Spread it so I can play with it."
"You are mine and I will do with you as I please."

Dominant Gestures

Dominant gestures signify ownership or power. For example, placing a collar around your partner's neck or putting them on a leash is a gesture of dominance. Submissive gestures might include averting your eyes when your dominant looks at you or getting on your knees when they are nearby.

Be a Good or Unruly Submissive

There are many ways to be a submissive, but the most important part is knowing that, ultimately, you have choice in the situation, and you can always use your safe word if your dominant does or says something that does not work for you. If it fits with your fantasy, let your dominant know what kinds of activities and words are most arousing to you. Once you know that you are choosing this and you have given your dominant all the information they need, you can truly let go and be taken on the journey.

You can be a very good submissive and do and say exactly what your dominant tells you to, or you can be unruly and fight back so that you get more punishments. Allow yourself to play with different roles. You can see what it is like to be completely silent and compliant. You can make loud noises and cause problems for your dominant, such as by squirming or running away, saying no, not doing what they say right away, or pushing back. After you play, take time to communicate and give feedback about how the experience was for you.

Exercise: Give Your Partner a Spanking

It is time to dip your toe in the waters of the dominant movie by giving your partner a spanking. First establish a safe word the submissive can use.

Then find a fun spanking position. Since you are in charge, you will need to get your partner into the position that is most arousing to you. You might say, "Lean over, put your hands on the table, and spread your legs." Or you might use a hair hold to guide them to the bed, push their face down, and say, "Stick your ass in the air for me." Or you might beckon them over and gently but firmly say, "Be a good girl and lie across my lap. It's time for your spanking."

Once you have your partner in a good position, make sure you are also positioned in a way that gives you the best spanking angle. You may need to experiment with this a bit, so be patient with yourself and each other as you learn. The first time you spank your partner, you will want to get an idea of their pain threshold. Try a light spank and have them tell you how painful it is on a scale from one to ten, where they can barely feel one and ten is right at the edge of what they can handle.

Danielle Harel PhD & Celeste Hirschman MA

With an idea of their pain threshold, you can try different approaches. You can work your way up slowly, from gentle smacks and pats to much more intense pain. Or you can start with a six or seven and give nice hard spanks interspersed with petting, teasing, and talking. See what you and your partner like best.

There are two main types of spanks that we have found to be the most arousing for the majority of people. These are slapping and cupping. Experiment with each of them to see if you like both or one much more than the other.

1. **Slapping**: A slapping spank is done with a flat hand and has follow-through. Slapping spanks create more of stinging feeling and usually make more noise. Try slapping your partner's ass with an upward swing and a downward swing. This will get different parts of their ass.
2. **Cupping:** Cup your hand and end the spank on your partner's ass cheek. Do not follow through. Instead, end the spank with a nice thud on your partner's ass. Cupping offers more of a deep, pounding feeling.

Some people plant a nice slap on their partner's ass and move on to the next spank or another part of the body, missing an amazing opportunity. Immediately after a spank, the blood has moved to the surface of your partner's ass cheek, leaving the spot you just spanked highly sensitized. Immediately after the slap, give the spot some feathery touch or slow, light scratches.

Throughout the spanking, make sure that you are giving each cheek equal attention. Also try varying the amount of time between spanks to increase your partner's uncertainty about when the next spank is going to come; this allows them to experience anticipation and the feeling that you are in charge.

Make sure to give feedback to each other after your spanking experience. If you are the submissive, tell your dominant what you really liked, and tell and demonstrate on their body anything you'd like to be different next time. If you are the dominant, tell your submissive what you loved about how they responded and what kinds of responses would arouse you even more.

Journal opportunity: Your Hottest Sexual Movie

Now that you have been introduced to the most common sexual movies, write down which aspects of the movies are most arousing to you. Write a specific paragraph or list of the kinds of story, energy, touch, words, and gestures that you like to fantasize about and a separate list of those you'd like to experience.

Understand Rape Fantasies

About 80% of women fantasize about rape. Let us be clear here: women **DO NOT** want to be raped. Rape fantasies allow women to navigate the impossible dilemma of having desires but being seen as sluts if they act on them. A rape fantasy provides a work-around to this dilemma. It frees a woman from responsibility for willingly engaging in the sexual experience. In a rape fantasy she has not made a conscious decision to have sex and therefore does not have to worry that she might be seen as a slut. In addition, rape fantasies allow a woman to safely explore her desire for aggressive sex. She can play with the idea of experiencing men's animalistic desires without experiencing the actual terror and pain that come from real rape. Some women even like to play these fantasies out with their partners in a safe and boundaried environment.

You might ask yourself, why would a woman fantasize about something she doesn't actually want to do? There are many reasons for this. In fantasies about rape the woman might actually imagine herself in the role of the man, therefore experiencing a sense of power she may have lost at an earlier time in her life when she felt powerless or violated. A woman might have a fantasy that is violating or painful that she doesn't want to actually enact; she simply *wants to feel the full force of her arousal.* Or a woman may have had a traumatic or less voluntary experience and now wants to reclaim her body and the experience in a safe environment with a trusted partner, gaining a sense of choice and power in a situation similar to the original experience, in which she had none.

Play with Roles

Playing with roles or "role play" is when you take on the character or personality of someone or something other than yourself—a person, an animal, or a superhero. It may involve dressing up as different characters or simply acting them out. Role playing is an opportunity to explore different parts of your personality that you might not have experienced before. For example, if you are usually more timid sexually, you might consider playing a porn star or a prostitute. If you feel like you are always in charge, you might see what it's like to play a young boy being seduced by his teacher. Role playing can be a great way to introduce psychological arousal into your sexual repertoire.

Role playing is a wonderful way that two consenting adults can play with fantasies. Role plays might be based on power differentials in age, gender, or social position. For example, you might role-play a doctor and patient or a young girl and the corrupting older brother of her best friend. Often role playing includes the breaking of a taboo as well as or instead of a power differential between the two characters. An example of a role play that breaks a taboo but doesn't include much of a power difference would be two teenagers discovering sex for the first time. When role-playing, it is important to commit fully to the role and take it seriously.

Role playing can bring up a lot of embarrassment, so you might need to practice with it a number of times to get comfortable. If you really dive in, it can be a very liberating experience.

The Spiritual Movie
Recently in the U.S. there has been a contingent of sexuality educators teaching "tantra," "neo-tantra," or "sacred sexuality." The idea behind these teachings is wonderful: that your sexuality is a sacred part of who you are and that its expression is an expression of your connection with your spiritual self.

You can see some elements of tantric teaching, such as breath work and the idea that sexuality is an energetic exchange, in this book. We want to emphasize that any practice of sexuality can be sacred. Two people's sharing of romance, passion, dominance/submission, or some combination of these can be profound and sacred. The sacredness of a sexual experience has more to do with the intention and connection of the actors than with the actions themselves.

This being said, for some people their Hottest Sexual Movie has an overt spiritual or sacred theme. The spiritual movie can include wanting to feel like or be treated like a god or goddess, worshipping your partner or being worshipped by them. It also means seeing each other as a representation of the divine. Spiritual sexuality focuses on breathing together; honoring each other through rituals such as dance, incense, and candle-lighting; intention-setting and conscious touch; and connection. Sexual acts in this movie often focus on the giving and receiving of sensual massage. They are intended to heal, build energy in the body, and bring full-body pleasure or orgasm as a way to connect with the divine.

The Fetish Movie

As a culture, we generally think of fetishes as some pathologized, weird desire that "those other people" have. However, some fetishes have been incorporated into the mainstream sexual repertoire and are not judged. For example, if you need your partner to wear high-heeled shoes or something lacy in order to get really turned on during sex, you may not even have to ask. Many women wear high heels and lace as part of their dating and sexual attire. These are socially accepted fetishes. It is somewhat more challenging for people whose sexual fetishes fall outside of cultural norms. As long as they don't cause anyone harm, we invite you to embrace your fetishes.

One example we saw in our office was a man, Ted, who was turned on only if his partner wore a cast on some part of her body—her leg, her arm, or even a foot or hand. Most of Ted's relationships had been very short, because he would try to have sex with a castless partner and be unable to get an erection. His partners felt rejected and he felt hopeless, like he would never find a woman who was okay with his desires.

When Ted came to see us, he was desperate. He had met a woman, Candace, whom he felt he wanted to marry. He told us she was everything he wanted in a partner, describing her as "down to earth, practical yet fun, and, for me, the definition of beauty and grace." They had been dating for three months and had fooled around but not yet had sex. Candace was from a religious background and was happy that Ted wanted to wait; he was glad the pressure was off long enough for him to really experience falling in love and feel his attachment to her and hers to him. He was terrified to tell her of his desires and afraid to ask her to come with him to see us: "We've only been dating for three months," he said, "and now I have to tell her I want her to come in for sex coaching. She's going to think I'm a freak."

It took us a while to help Ted understand that there was nothing wrong with his sexual desires, that they had developed a long time ago, likely as a result of a forgotten early-childhood experience of someone with a cast or of being in one himself. As we talked through it, he saw that we were not judgmental. He realized that there were many people out there with fetishes and that some very common fetishes had even been incorporated into the mainstream. As we continued to normalize his need for a cast, we also let Ted know that Candace would likely be surprised, maybe even upset or uncomfortable at first. We helped him decide whether or not he wanted to tell her and offered other options, such as using Cialis. We also helped him wrestle with the fact that, if he did decide to share, it might take a while for her to accept him, and that ultimately she might not. In the end, he decided that he wanted to find someone who could love all of him, as he had learned to do for himself, so he told her.

The Sensation Movie

Some people's psychological and physiological arousal are so closely connected that they would probably say they do not fantasize at all. If your arousal seems to come completely from physical touch and sensation, then you are probably most interested in what we call the sensation movie. For one woman we worked with, the sensation of water on her body from a shower, pool, or hot tub was central to her arousal. When she was in the water, she felt caressed, surrounded, held, and weightless. You can see how these feelings are both physiological and psychological. Though this movie does not fit into a traditional definition of a fantasy, it is a rich, wonderful fantasy.

Whether sensation is your whole movie or just an enhancement of the psychological arousal you get from sex, your sex life will likely improve if you pay attention to what kinds of sensations and stimulation you want and then share that information with your partner. Being blindfolded and then having your partner bring many kinds of different sensations to your body is a great way to focus on sensation and learn about what you like. Remember that touch, taste, smell, and sound are all sensations you can offer or receive in an erotic experience.

Try these with your partner:

- Caressing with feathers and silk scarves
- Feeding your partner chocolate or strawberries dipped in whipped cream

- Placing an ice cube directly on your partner's body, or putting it in your mouth to make your lips and tongue cold, then kissing and licking your partner's body
- Using warm water on your lips and tongue to alternate between cold kisses and warm ones
- Playing the kind of music or sound that gets your partner most in the mood, or breathing or whispering in their ear

Combine Movies and Bring Sensuality

Your greatest fulfillment as a couple will come from some beautiful combination of these movies and your own unique spin on them. When you combine different sexual attitudes and sensual skills, like animalistic ass grabbing with light kisses down the back of the neck, your sex life will stay new and exciting. In any sexual experience you can move between overt passion, slow seduction, and play with power roles, allowing arousal to really grow. When you take the time to play and build, you will likely have more connection, greater intimacy, and many more orgasms. Be creative, be spontaneous, and be patient—finding the experiences that work well for you and your partner takes time.

Tease and Tantalize the Body

No matter what movie or combination of movies you do, it is essential to warm up and tantalize the body throughout the experience.

Making love to your partner is like playing a symphony; you have to create a foundation of sound before you can move to the powerful crescendos. When you give the body enough time for a foundation of sensation to build, you set the stage for extraordinary passion and explosive orgasms and multi-orgasms. Any sexual encounter is enhanced by warming up the whole body instead of rushing straight to the genitals. In fact, while light touching on the cock can be nice for a man at the beginning of a sexual encounter, touching a woman's clitoris or G-spot too soon can have a numbing effect, making it take longer for her to get aroused and orgasm than it would have if you had warmed her up more before touching her pussy.

Move from Periphery to Center

When you start a sexual encounter with a woman, begin with the periphery and move to the center. Think of the "center" as her pussy and breasts (and asshole if that is part of your sex play) and the rest of her body as the "periphery." When you move from periphery to center, each stroke and touch and squeeze on other parts of her body sends teasing messages to her pussy, creating anticipation and saying, "I'll be there soon, you just have to wait for me…" When you move from periphery to center, you give her pussy time to get aroused, warm up, and lubricate. Men often gain a lot of arousal by touching their partners. They can have much more intense pleasure if they get touch all over their bodies as well. Whether you are touching a man or a woman, it is important not to focus solely on the genitals.

Caress the Entire Body

Use long strokes and all-over-body touch that includes the hair, arms, back, legs, butt, and stomach. Remember, desires can change over the course of a month, a day, or even a single sexual experience. Be open to changes in what turns each of you on and approach each experience with communication and an open mind.

Stroke the hair. Having your hair touched can be both soothing and very arousing. When you touch your partner's hair, either stroke over it or run your fingers through it like a comb; everyone likes their hair touched and stroked differently.

Nibble and bite the neck and ears. Start with kisses and light bites on your partner's neck and ears. Focus especially on the back of the neck and shoulders for biting. Some people really like blowing and licking around their ears, but others find it irritating—notice body language and cues, and when in doubt, ask!

Tantalize the back. The back loves long, slow, feathery touches, especially around the upper back and neck and along the sides of the torso, waist, and hips. When you run your fingers across your partner's back, make sure to give feather touch to the back of the neck.

Tease the thighs. The thighs, especially the inner thighs, offer a great opportunity for teasing, as you can get close to the cock or pussy without touching it. This increases anticipation and can help a woman love her thighs. Run your fingers or tongue up the inner thighs.

Include the stomach. Many people, especially women, do not feel comfortable with the size or shape of their stomach. No matter how it looks to you, your partner may feel that their belly is too big. Helping your partner love their stomach will help them relax and breathe down more deeply so they can connect with their pussy or cock. Positive verbal messages about your partner's stomach, combined with touches, kisses, nibbles, and licks, will help them to love and integrate this part of their body.

Touch the belly lightly, kiss and caress it, lick circles around the bellybutton. Move to the horizontal line where the stomach ends and the pelvis begins—this is a very sensitive area that can enjoy feather touch and light licking.

Pay special attention to the hot spots. Most people have certain places that are more sensitive. Common hot spots are the backs of the knees and inner elbows, the armpits, the back of the neck, under and around the sides of the breasts/chest, the lower part of the stomach near the underwear line, the sides of the body, the inner thighs, the ass cheeks, and the toes. Take time to visit each of these hot spots, exploring them slowly with your hands, lips, tongue, and teeth.

Explore the armpits. Armpits can be particularly powerful areas for exploration because they have so many nerve endings and rarely receive touch. If your partner is not wearing deodorant and is not too ticklish, try touching, licking, biting, and smelling their armpits. If going directly to the pit is too intense for you, try licking around the edges where there is no hair.

Experience the breasts/chest. For many women and some men, the breasts/chest and especially the nipples can be very sensitive. Take some time to share with your partner how you like your breasts/chest and nipples touched. When touching your partner's breasts/chest, stroke around the sides and underneath before moving to the nipples. This gives the body the powerful message that you are willing to take your time and build towards pleasure. At the beginning of a sexual encounter, your breasts/chest might enjoy feather touch, licking, blowing air, and brushing of the fingers across the nipple. Once you get warmed up, you may like nipple pinching, twisting, or pulling. The breasts/chest/nipples are a great place to use ice and warm water.

Exercise: Receive Actively
In a sexual situation, people are often busy thinking about how to please their partner. As a result, they don't take the time to sink in and feel what is happening to their body. Actively receiving is about putting your full attention on your bodily responses and focusing on your inner experiences as opposed to trying to give at the same time as you receive.

Take at least a half hour to allow your partner to touch your body while you just receive. Then switch roles and try again. This is a great time to map some of your hot spots. When you are in the receiving role, you don't have to do *anything* to reciprocate! Just receive and absorb your partner's touch—a challenge if you are one of the many people for whom it is very difficult to relax. Active receiving means lying back and enjoying, but it is by no means passive.

To receive actively, one partner at a time should follow these 5 steps:

1. Get in a comfortable position where you feel relaxed and ready to receive. This may be lying on your stomach or your back, sitting on the couch, or even standing up—whatever feels good to you.
2. Begin doing embodiment breathing, focusing all of your attention inwardly, towards your own erotic energy, your

cock or pussy, and your skin, where you will be feeling the sensations.

3. Have your partner begin to touch your body, and take some time to relax into the touch. Allow yourself and your partner to sink into the experience without giving any direction. After a few minutes, you may want to give a little bit of direction, but your partner should still keep the focus on sinking into the sensations and enjoying giving touch. Try not to pop either of you out of the experience and into your head by talking too much.

4. As you feel the sensations on your body, allow it to respond in ways that feel good to you. You might respond with movement, breath, and sounds. Moans or "mmmmms" or words such as "yes" and "I like that" or "That feels good" are great. You can also touch your own body as you are being touched if that enhances your arousal. This is not about forcing a response or putting on a show but about letting go of shame. Shame causes people to minimize their expressions of pleasure, especially their voice. For many of our clients, opening the vocal cords to allow sounds or words is one of the hardest things to do. But making sounds can greatly enhance your pleasure, spread erotic energy throughout your body, and intensify orgasm. Let yourself make some noise—if the neighbors hear, perhaps you will be an inspiration to them! If your children hear something, they will know their parents really like each other.

5. As you are receiving touch all over your body, connect with your pussy or cock from the inside. This may mean doing some pelvic floor muscle squeezes (also called Kegel exercises) or just imagining that all of the pleasure is spreading across your body and through your pelvic

floor. This will help you build arousal and stay engrossed in the experience.

Give Each Other Amazing Orgasms

While we do not want to encourage a goal-oriented approach, the fact is that people love their orgasms. To reach the heights of orgasmic pleasure, you will need to understand each other's desires and bodies and use all of your tools. In the following sections you will learn all about women's and men's orgasms, the physiology of pleasure and what kinds of touch and stimulation will lead to your best orgasms ever.

Understand and Expand Women's Orgasms

Women's capacity for pleasure and orgasms is endless. While this sounds very promising, it can cause performance anxiety for many women, who worry that they need to have every type of orgasm, be able to ejaculate, etc. Women also fear that they take too long; while men are often trying to hold off their orgasms as long as possible, women are generally rushing to the finish.

Women worry that men won't appreciate them as sexual partners if they don't have orgasms quickly enough or the way they think men want them to (i.e., during intercourse or without a vibrator).

Throughout history women suffered from sexual oppression and limitation around their orgasms; they were told that something was wrong with them if they couldn't have what Freud referred to as "vaginal orgasms" and that clitoral orgasms were "immature." The pressure can lead women to fake orgasms, making it even less likely that their partners will learn how to please them. We invite you to let go of the hierarchy of orgasms. Appreciate them however and whenever they come in a sexual experience. Women need to be able to have their choice around orgasm, as some might not want the pressure to orgasm every time they have sex.

The Damaging Myth of the Proper Orgasm

There are three parts to the damaging myth of the proper orgasm, each of which puts pressure on women and couples to have the right kind of orgasm instead of celebrating every orgasm and all the different kinds of pleasure that are possible during sex. The first is that women are supposed to have unassisted orgasms during intercourse. The second is that women are supposed to orgasm without the use of a vibrator, and the third is that true connection is demonstrated by couples having simultaneous orgasms.

It bears repeating that 70 percent of women need clitoral stimulation in order to orgasm. This means that female orgasms during intercourse without the assistance of their hands, their partner's hands, or a vibrator can be quite rare, and the pressure to have them means that women end up experiencing much less pleasure during intercourse than they could. It also means that many women end up faking at least some of their orgasms. The inability to have orgasms during intercourse, if intercourse is the only kind of stimulation they are getting, will mean that sex isn't much fun. Faking orgasms can feel like lying and can cause very painful situations down the line, when women realize that they actually need to let their partner know that they are not having orgasms.

For some women the only way to attain orgasm is with a vibrator, and for others using a vibrator during sex makes orgasm and multi-orgasm exponentially easier and more likely. Sadly, many women are afraid to bring vibrators into the bedroom, and for some this means forgoing orgasms during sex or having them only occasionally or during solo masturbation. There are some common reasons why women deny themselves this pleasurable treat. They are afraid that they might hurt their partner's ego, fearing their partner might think, "Does this mean I'm not a good enough lover?" They fear that something is wrong with them if they need a vibrator to come. They feel (or fear that their partner feels) that vibrators are not "natural." They are afraid that they will become addicted to vibrators and not be able to have orgasms through other sexual experiences.

In response, here are some of our personal and professional thoughts about vibrators. Using a vibrator during sex is as "natural" as eating with a fork or spoon. If we still did everything "naturally," we'd be living in caves and eating nothing but raw meat and berries. In the age of electricity and batteries, why not use some buzz to make your sex life more fulfilling? When a woman uses a vibrator, it does not make her partner obsolete, and any woman will tell you that using a vibrator with a partner is completely different and much more intense than using one alone.

Using a vibrator frees your partner up to bring the kind of presence and touch that will help you have the most intense, powerful, and pleasurable sexual experiences you have ever had. When a woman is using her vibrator, her partner can also use hands, fingers, cock, dildo, tongue, teeth, eye contact, and words to drive her wild. With the vibrator's help, a woman is much more likely to enjoy many orgasms instead of focusing all her attention to squeeze one little one out or, worse, to fake one. As for the fear that vibrators might be addictive, studies have shown that this simply is not the case.

The final part of the myth of the proper orgasm is that the ultimate orgasmic experience is simultaneous orgasms. While this can be a fun experience, it is merely one of many fun, mind-blowing, and exciting experiences you can have during sex. In reality it is rare for two people to have the same arousal curves and orgasmic timing. Generally men get aroused more quickly than women, and often they try to learn to last long enough for their partner to orgasm. If you have trouble lasting long enough, another option is to assist a woman with her orgasms after you come. Women can be multi-orgasmic, so trying to synchronize orgasms might mean that she has only one when she could have many more.

Accept and celebrate who you and your partner are as sexual beings and all of the pleasure you experience during sex, regardless of whether you are having orgasms. Embrace and feel proud of the orgasms you and your partner have, no matter from whence they come.

Types of Female Orgasm

The three major types of female orgasms—clitoral, G-Spot, and cervical—each travel across a different set of nerves and therefore create different sensations in the body. Women can also have combination orgasms, where two or three of the neural pathways are activated. Below we explore how you can best help a woman reach each of these different types of orgasm.

Clitoral Orgasms

As mentioned above, up to 70 percent of women need some type of clitoral stimulation in order to orgasm. Some women like direct touch on their clit, while many women's clits are very sensitive and need the protection of the clitoral hood, especially when they are first being touched.

As a woman, you can tell your partner how you like to be touched or show them how you masturbate. If you are watching a woman masturbate, pay close attention to the touch she is giving her vulva, including her clitoris and vaginal opening. Notice how she rubs her clit—pay attention especially to the direction, pressure, speed, and timing.

To warm up the pussy, hold, tease, and tickle. Begin by holding her whole pussy, cupping your hand such that your middle finger is near her perineum and the palm of your hand is on her mons. After cupping, move to feather touch across her entire vulva.

When first approaching the clit, use a very light touch, and anytime you are touching it, use the soft pads of at least three of your fingers instead of your fingertips. This gives you more coverage, making it more likely that you will stimulate the most sensitive parts of her clit. When you are still bringing her arousal up, be playful and creative, visiting the clit and then moving away so that the anticipation continues to build.

Once she gets close to orgasm (which is often signaled non-verbally through clenching muscles, holding breath, and/or making sounds), stop being creative and continue doing exactly what you were doing when she started getting close. Do exactly that until she comes.

Try the Three Basic Moves

Women who masturbate using their hands move their fingers up and down, side to side, or in circles across their pussy. These are the three basic strokes. You can begin by doing any of them slowly and lightly using longer strokes, then move faster and add pressure as her arousal increases. When you add more pressure and move your hand faster, your strokes may get shorter. Make sure to get a lot of friction and motion across the clit. Be careful that adding pressure does not stop you from getting enough coverage or friction. Move across the clit rather than moving the clit around.

Discover Advanced Clit Play

The Taco: Squeeze her outer lips so that they snugly surround the clit; this makes the clit pop out a bit. Now you can brush across it lightly with your fingers, stroking from the vagina up to the mons, side to side, or in circles.

The Anchor: Anchor two fingers so that one is on either side of the clit, between the inner and outer lips. Move the fingers in very small vibrating motions so that the clit feels the vibration.

Party Time: For many women the two o'clock point or the ten o'clock point on the clit can be very pleasurable due to additional nerve bundles in those locations. You might try focusing your stimulation at these points and see if you get more response.

Consider introducing a vibrator into your sex play, especially if extended stimulation, lots of pressure, or very quick motions are needed. As a woman, it is better to drive your own vibrator than to let your partner do it, as you will be able to adjust instantly based on how the stimulation feels. Meanwhile, their hands will be free to touch you all over or stimulate your G-spot.

Finding a good vibrator is a matter of trial and error. The Hitachi Magic Wand is a favorite because of its deep, penetrating vibrations. However, it is very strong. Try using a washcloth between your vulva and the vibrator when you first try it, and make sure you are warmed up. The Magic Wand is good for doggie-style intercourse or during sex in a spooning position. The Mystic Wand is a smaller, slightly less intense version of the Magic Wand and can be a good alternative. There are also many new vibrators that are much smaller and flatter but still quite strong. If you enjoy missionary position, smaller, flatter vibrators are a great choice for stimulation during intercourse, and they have graduated settings so you can go from light to more intense vibrations.

Multiple Orgasms

Women, if you are not already multi-orgasmic, you can probably become multi-orgasmic with some work. If you have never experienced multi-orgasms, you might assume that this first orgasm is the end of your sexual journey. You may even feel satisfied enough and not want to go on. But why not give it a try? You may find a whole new level of satisfaction you never knew was possible.

After your first clitoral orgasm, your clitoris may initially be very sensitive. If so, the last thing you want is for it to be touched or stimulated in any way.

If your clit needs a break after the first orgasm, have your partner cup your vulva with their whole hand—this will help to ground your body. After ten to thirty seconds, your clitoris should lose the intense sensitivity and you can enjoy a new wave of pleasure through clitoral stimulation. Start light and gradually build up touch as your body can handle more. If you find yourself a bit ticklish at first, lower the intensity of touch or go back to a holding touch for a few breaths. Subsequent orgasms often happen faster and can be closer together, which means a lot more payoff for a lot less effort.

G-Spot Orgasms

Some people say that women reach their sexual peak at forty. While this is not hormonally accurate, we believe it might be particularly true for women who discover G-spot pleasure later in life. G-spot stimulation can add a whole new level of pleasure to your sex life, substantially increasing your orgasmic potential.

The most important piece of information that you and your partner need to know about the G-spot is that its capacity for sensation develops throughout a woman's lifetime. Some women believe that they don't have a G-spot because, when the area is touched, they don't feel immediate sensation or arousal. They may even feel some irritation. This just means that the G-spot has not yet been developed to its full potential. To awaken, the G-spot needs to be massaged and given focused stimulation over time.

The G-spot is located right past the pelvic bone on the upper wall of the vagina. You can locate your partner's G-spot by placing one or two fingers inside the vagina a bit beyond your second knuckle and then bending your fingers in a "Come here" gesture. There does not need to be much in and out motion; just curling and uncurling the fingers does the trick. Remember, if her pussy is not wet, don't penetrate it. Women's capacity for lubrication changes throughout their lifetime and their menstrual cycle, and just because they aren't wet doesn't mean they are not aroused. Check with your partner about her lubrication. If she does not lubricate easily on her own, keep a lubricant nearby. Lubricants with a pump spout are best because they are easy access.

You can both get a good idea of what the G-spot feels like by doing the following: Put your tongue on the roof of your mouth right behind your teeth. Move the tip of tongue slightly inward and feel the bumpy part of the roof of your mouth. If you go a little farther back into your mouth with your tongue, there is a smooth area. Inside the vagina there is a rough area first; this is called the urethral sponge. Deeper inside the vagina is a smooth area. Pressure from your partner's fingers on the smooth area gives the best G-spot sensation.

In a small percentage of women, the G-spot develops early and becomes a place where they feel a lot of sensation. However, for many women the G-spot has not yet been developed, and it can take weeks or sometimes even a year of consistent stimulation to feel pleasure from it. Unfortunately, because many women have been told that the G-spot is a myth, when they feel numbness or irritation from G-spot stimulation, they give up and don't continue to explore the pleasure that may be available.

During penetration, a cock or dildo brushes across the G-spot. However, if the G-spot has not been awakened at all, this is unlikely to provide enough pressure and stimulation. Beginning with fingers has two perks. First, your partner can try out a wide range of pressures, starting gently and slowly working up to deeper, faster, more intense forms of stimulation.

Second, fingers are very sensitive and can map the most responsive locations on or around the G-spot. Having your partner massage the G-spot while applying increasing pressure, speed, and intensity is the surest way to awaken and arouse the G-spot, particularly if you remember to breathe and relax and accept that it may not happen right away.

When massaged patiently, the G-spot grows and expands. Pressure on it might make you feel like you need to pee. Many women are worried and embarrassed that they might pee on their partner, so they hold back at the most important pre-orgasmic moment, tightening up instead of letting go. This stops them from experiencing the depth of intensity that the G-spot can provide. If you can open up and let go in this moment, you have the opportunity for a G-spot orgasm, and you may also ejaculate at the same time.

G-spot orgasms are most commonly brought on when you open and relax your body or push down and out as if trying to pee. G-spot orgasms can be extremely intense and are more likely than clitoral orgasms to spread throughout your whole body. When exploring your G-spot, it is essential to have your partner warm up your body and pussy first. If you commonly have orgasms through clitoral stimulation, try having at least one clitoral orgasm before beginning your G-spot exploration.

Once you begin exploring the G-spot, your clitoris might become less sensitive and/or more difficult to locate. In your G-spot explorations, give yourself plenty of time (at least an hour) and remember that you don't need to try to orgasm or ejaculate. Simply be receptive and feel into what sensations are possible for you. Have your partner go slowly and lightly and then build speed and pressure. Make sure your partner tries lots of different strokes, speeds, and pressures. Give feedback about what feels best for you. Don't forget, this is likely to change over the course of a day and over the weeks, months, and years of your life. As you become more aroused, you will generally be able to take more pressure. You may need a lot of pressure to orgasm from your G-spot, or you may respond to lighter touch.

Work your way back. It is best to start with fingertips at the opening of the vagina and make slow circles. Try different pressures and speeds with lots of feedback. Continue with slow circles at the opening, then across the bumpy part, and finally directly on the G-spot.

Come hither. The most effective G-spot maneuver is the "come hither" motion, where your partner pulls one, two, or three fingers across the G-spot. Some women like the "come here" motion right on top of the bumpy part, while others prefer it on the smoother part just past the pubic bone. If they are on the right spot, they will be able to hook their fingers behind your pubic bone.

Tap. Have your partner insert their fingers and tap directly on the G-spot. They can start gently and work their way up, seeing how much pressure it can take. They can also vary the speed.

Get noisy. One way to get more sensation from your G-spot is to make sounds while it is being stimulated; this helps relax the muscles in your vagina and allows you to move towards orgasm. For some women, G-spot stimulation and orgasms can be very emotional; you may cry, laugh, or scream. Both of you should stay present for whatever arises, including any emotion that may come up—from joyous ecstasy to tears or a combination of the two.

Uterine or Cervical Orgasms

One woman we worked with said her uterine orgasm felt like someone was ringing a big bell inside her, and she said, "I felt like that bell was still ringing for three days afterwards." Cervical orgasms can be extremely intense and happen when fingers or a cock or dildo presses on or around the cervix. The cervix protrudes into the vagina. Pressure can be applied directly on the protruding area or to the moat around the edge of the cervix.

You may like direct stimulation on or across the cervix. You may be more aroused when fingers are circling your cervix or when you are receiving thrusting pressure around the edge in the moat. Often there is one area that is most sensitive, and this location can shift and move throughout your cycle and your life.

Combination Orgasms

Any of these orgasms can be combined for a greater intensification of pleasure. Vibrators can be great for combination orgasms. For example, you might have your partner stimulate your G-spot and/or cervix while you use a vibrator on your clit.

Oral Sex on a Woman

In combination with the all-over body caressing and warming up that we've described above, oral sex can be a complete sex act in and of itself—either giving or receiving or both. If you have watched porn, you have likely had extensive lessons in how *not* to lick a pussy, as the actors dive right to the clit with hard, direct licking. Oral sex needs slow build-up and savoring.

Some women don't like oral sex. If you are a woman who does not like oral sex because you feel ashamed or embarrassed about your pussy and the way it looks, smells, or tastes, it might be helpful for you to do some work on your pussy image. You can let your partner lick you and tell you how delicious your pussy tastes and smells. Learning to love your pussy may take time, but it's worth it! If you are someone who wants to give oral sex but is reluctant due to sensitivity to tastes, smells, or messiness, try licking or kissing over the panties and make sure your partner takes a bath or shower before you give her oral sex.

If you are comfortable with your pussy, you still might not like oral sex because you are not clit-oriented. Some women orgasm solely from other parts of their body, like their G-spot, cervix, ass, or nipples. You can go down on this type of a woman for hours and never get her any closer to an orgasm. If your partner is a woman who does not get much from oral stimulation of the pussy but you really love to give oral sex, you may still be able to negotiate some pussy licking. Tell her that you just want to do it for a while and you'd love for her to relax and enjoy, with no pressure to orgasm. Many women who don't come through oral stimulation still find it pleasurable or arousing. Also remember that women's comfort, bodies, and desires change throughout their lives. Even if you are a woman who doesn't want oral sex now, you can occasionally give it a try and see if you change your mind.

Usually women who like oral sex like it a lot. This means that as the giver it is important to take your time. Oral sex offers a lot of direct clitoral stimulation, and using your tongue can be a great way to bring her to orgasm, but it's important to warm up her body first. Then you can begin to move towards her pussy, taking your time and lingering on some of the more sensitive areas we discussed, especially the lower part of her stomach and her inner thighs. When you first make contact, keep in mind that it is still all about sensual creativity and teasing.

One excellent transition into oral sex is to go from kissing her thighs and stomach to placing light, teasing kisses on her pussy. Because kisses represent love and affection, kissing is a wonderful way to show her pussy how much you desire it and appreciate it while continuing the tease. Cover her whole pussy with soft kisses, including her mons and lips, being very gentle near the clit. Remember, you can always move to heavier, more direct pressure later, but if you bring it in too quickly you will miss an opportunity to drive her crazy with your teasing.

Another wonderful approach to teasing is to think of her pussy as a delicious ice cream cone. Keep your tongue soft, wide, and flat, just as you would if you were licking ice cream, and begin with long, slow, light, sensual licks from the bottom of the pussy to the top. In addition to the ice-cream-cone lick, you can also suck gently or more vigorously on her outer lips or her inner lips if they are large enough. Also try sliding your tongue between her inner and outer lips before you apply direct touch and pressure to her clit.

Once you do move to the clit, the basic strokes are up and down, side to side, and circles. Begin slowly and then gradually increase your speed and pressure.

It is possible to get lost in the pussy and to forget about the other parts of her body. Continuing manual touch on her thighs, stomach, breasts, and nipples can heighten sensation and pleasure and help bring her to orgasm. Try stroking her hips, pinching her nipples, or adding G-spot stimulation to increase her overall sensation..

Pay attention to her nonverbal cues. If she is pulling her pelvis away from you, she likely needs lighter pressure, while grabbing your head or pushing her pelvis towards you is probably a sign she needs more pressure. Another important cue is how she is moving her hips. Sadly, for women it is sometimes still difficult to simply say, "A little to the left." Instead, they move their hips a little to the right, hoping you will stay put. Some men are so engrossed in what they are doing that they follow the pussy around wherever it goes and miss this nonverbal cue completely. If she is moving to the left, she needs you to be more to the right; if she's moving her hips up, she needs your tongue lower down; if she's moving her hips down, she needs it higher up.

If she is wildly thrusting her pelvis about and you can't seem to stay connected with her clit, just keep your tongue flat and available and let her rub herself across it. There are some great variations you can bring to the picture by adding anchoring, suction, and light nibbling and biting. If her clitoral shaft is big enough, you can anchor her clit by wrapping your lips around it so that you can hold it in place. When you have it anchored with your lips, lick the clit with up-and-down, side-to-side, or circular motions. Anchoring the shaft gives increased sensation because both the sides of her clitoral shaft and the head of her clit are getting stimulation. From the anchored position, you can also add light suction to the mix, sucking the clit between your lips, then releasing and sucking again.

You can also move your lips up and down along the shaft, kind of like a clitoral blow job. Suction pulls more blood into the clit and can really increase sensation. You can also try nibbling gently with your teeth or running them lightly up and down her clitoral shaft. As she gets closer to coming, she will usually breathe faster and may even help you out with words such as "Don't stop," "I'm going to cum," or "Yes, just like that." At this point you need to completely let go of creativity, allow her to get you to the right location and pressure, and keep doing exactly what you are doing.

Women's orgasms can be elusive; a slight change in rhythm, direction, or pressure at this moment and you may have to go all the way back to the start. No matter what she does—if she is bucking, squeezing your face, or suffocating you—as long as you aren't going to die, just keep doing what you are doing until you feel her release.

During oral sex, some women like to have a finger in their vagina, their asshole, or both for increased pleasure and sensation and the potential for combination orgasms. You can also incorporate stimulation of her nipples or cervix and see if this enhances her pleasure or leads to combination orgasm. Women who orgasm solely from their clit might be distracted by the insertion of a finger. If she pulls away when you try to insert a finger, stops making sounds, or seems to relax her body and move away from orgasm, take your finger back out.

Women who like manual G-spot, cervical, or anal stimulation can be extremely pleased by combining them with oral sex. This may be what they need to take them to new heights or bring them over the edge. Don't forget to use different fingers for the asshole and the vagina, so as not to cause a bacterial infection, and always use lube for anal insertion. When introducing a finger, take it slow; at first simply tease your fingers over her asshole or the lips of her vagina. Then try inserting a finger into her vagina, her ass, or both.

Whether your fingers are in her ass or her vagina, you can try hooking them upward and giving the "come here" motion to stimulate her G-spot or thrusting them in and out to give her more of a "fucking" feeling. If you go all the way into her vagina during oral sex, you can also stimulate her on or around her cervix. All of these bring the possibility of increased pleasure and sensation and combination orgasms.

Journal opportunity: Women's Orgasms
Women: write about the kinds of orgasms you have had or think you have had. Write about the most common ways you feel like you get them.

If your partner is a woman: write about the the kinds of orgasmsyour partner has had or you think they have had. Write about the most common ways you feel like they get them.

Expand Men's Orgasms

While men's orgasms are generally more straight-forward than women's, you will still want to give your partner a variety of touch, including different strokes and amounts of pressure. Enthusiasm, passion and creativity around his cock will make all the difference between an okay orgasm and an Oh-My-God orgasm.

The Damaging Myths About Men's Sexual Response

Before going into the details of how to give your man amazing orgasms, you want to be aware of the damaging myths that affect men's sexuality. Many of these have to do with expectations about performance. The first myth that gets in the way of men having good sex is the idea that they are supposed to be interested in and ready for sex all the time.

There are many reasons why men don't want to have sex all the time or why they develop sexual dysfunction. They can be exhausted and overworked, or they might be tired of feeling rejected after initiating sex. They might also be responding to a feeling of distance or a lot of anger directed at them if they don't want sex or are unable to perform.

For example, Chad and Lila had been married four years when Chad came to us complaining of erectile dysfunction. Chad told us, "Sometimes Lila approaches me and she's all hot and horny and I just can't get into it. I feel like such a loser. I'm letting her down all the time." We quickly discovered, however, that he was working an average of eighty hours per week and training for a marathon. We were surprised that he wanted sex at all. Chad is an extreme case, but as men get older, it is normal for them to want sex less often, especially if they have very taxing and stressful lives. It is important that men be able say no to sex in their relationships when they are not in the mood.

Chad also told us that his wife was very particular about how she wanted to be seduced and touched. He shared with us that whenever he did something to her sexually that she didn't like, she started yelling at him. He said, "She just looks at me with annoyance on her face and says things like 'Real men can get it up' and 'My ex-boyfriend knew exactly what to do without me having to tell him.' Most of the time, no matter what I do, she just lays there, and I have no idea what she likes and doesn't like." When it came to their sex life, he felt helpless, frustrated, and rejected. We were not at all surprised that he was having trouble getting an erection. This is not dysfunction. This situation and others like it are a functional response to a dysfunctional situation. Chad's body was responding properly to what was happening to him: his cock didn't want to go inside someone who was mean and abusive to him.

The second myth is that men are supposed to get hard as soon as any kind of sexual play has been initiated and remain hard throughout the sexual experience. However, after men's teenage hormonal peak (and sometimes even during it, depending on what kinds of sexual messages and experiences they've had), the ability to maintain an erection fluctuates. As men age, they need more direct stimulation on their cocks to get hard and stay hard.

Most physically healthy men who are not having a functional response to a dysfunctional situation experience erections that go up and down during a single sexual experience. Most men also periodically have experiences of not being able to get an erection. When you think that something is wrong with you if you don't get an erection, you can go into a state of performance anxiety, which then makes the erection less likely to return. The more you accept that your erection may go up and down during a sexual experience, and the more your partners don't take it personally, the more likely you are to be able to enjoy the entire erotic experience and the less likely you are to end up with an ongoing case of erectile dysfunction.

In addition to feeling pressure to get hard, men (especially men who have sex with women) also feel pressure to last a long time. Because there is a big difference in the average amount of time it takes men and women to orgasm, women put pressure on themselves to orgasm quickly and men put pressure on themselves to last longer. There is no "right" amount of time it should take to have an orgasm, but the difference causes a lot of performance anxiety for both men and women. We have worked with many men to help them to learn to control their ejaculation, and we are sometimes surprised at the calls we get. We asked one man, who called with a self-described ejaculation control issue, how long it usually takes him to orgasm. "I usually come in about a half an hour," he said, "but I really want to be able to please my partner fully." He was relieved to hear that the average amount of time men last is about seven minutes and that many women prefer a much more varied sex life and wouldn't want to have intercourse for longer than he could last.

The final damaging myth is that men are supposed to ejaculate on command. The truth is that men sometimes have difficulty climaxing, and this is normal. For some, certain sexual acts are much more likely to bring them to climax than others. Some men will need to masturbate at least some of the time in order to ejaculate. When men feel ready to orgasm or feel like their partner wants them to orgasm more quickly, one or both partners may go into "work mode," where they are working hard trying to get to orgasm. This is generally frustrating, isn't sexy, and usually causes the orgasm to get further and further away. It can be very helpful to remove the pressure on men to come on command or come through specific sexual acts. Sex can be very pleasurable for men regardless of whether they ejaculate, and if they need to give themselves a helping hand, it can be very hot to experience a man coming on your body.

Cocks

While most women want a good amount of warm-up before their pussies get touched, men might like their cock touched as part of their warm-up. Men should tell their partner when they'd like their cock to be touched. Some men feel very warmed up by touching their partner's body, but it is also wonderful to reciprocate and give all-over-body touch to your male partner. You can touch him on his arms, shoulders, chest, and stomach before making your way down to his cock.

Sadly, most cocks get touched one way. Men's partners grab the shaft, firmly grip it, and slide their hand up and down. While this can be arousing, cocks, just like pussies, can have much more heightened sensation if they get approached in varied ways. For example, you might start by gently running your fingers along the shaft and balls, tickling the balls lightly, and teasing the head of the cock with your fingertips. It can be as nice to tease a soft cock as a hard one. Teasing is a wonderful way to coax a cock into arousal without as much pressure. The more you let yourself enjoy the texture of the skin and the gliding motion, the more relaxing and arousing it is.

If you are with someone who is uncircumcised and you want to start bringing in firmer touch, start by using your hand to slide the foreskin up and down on the head of the cock. The foreskin is like a built-in lubrication system, moisturizing and protecting the sensitive head of the cock. If you are with a circumcised man or are going to touch the head of an uncircumcised man's cock directly, you might want to use some massage oil, coconut oil, or lube. Some kind of oil is generally better than lube for cocks, but make sure that you don't use oil if you will be using condoms later, because it will weaken the condom and cause it to break. If you don't have anything around, you can always improvise by putting some spit on your hand. Whether or not he is circumcised, you can enhance the sensation by pulling the skin of the cock down towards the base. Pulling the skin tight on the cock brings the nerve endings closer to the surface, so touch will feel more intense.

Simply wrapping your hand around the cock and moving it up and down is the basic stroke. You can play with different speeds and pressures. In general, you will want to use slower, lighter strokes to build anticipation and go faster and harder to move towards orgasm. The amount of pressure and the types of touch that are most pleasurable vary greatly from man to man. Men, try masturbating in front of your partner to show them how you like to be touched. Partners, when you watch him masturbate in front of you, pay attention to how he is touching himself. He may make full strokes up and down the shaft, rarely or never going across the head, or he may use short strokes focused mostly on the head. He may use a lot of pressure or may give his cock very light strokes. Watch how he plays with himself and see if you can mimic the way he touches himself at least part of the time you are touching him. If you are trying to bring him to orgasm with your hand, this will likely be the most efficient stroke.

Advanced Cock Strokes

There are many ways you can stroke a cock. Here are a few to experiment with, but definitely try making up your own ideas as well.

Tornado: Make sure your hand is nice and oily or wet. Place the palm of your hand on the frenulum (the area right below the head of the penis that is facing upwards when a man lies on his back and his penis is resting on his belly) and wrap your fingers around the top of the shaft and the head of the cock and apply some pressure. Now begin to rotate your wrist in circles so that your palm and fingers are sliding across the cock from side to side.

Head caresses: Use the wet or oily pads of your fingertips to glide across and tease the head of the cock, like you are gently coaxing and pulling the head. Roll the head between your fingertips.

Cock and balls: Make a circle around the top of the scrotum like a rubber band and pull the balls down and taut. (Men, let your partner know how far to pull to get maximum pleasure.) Use your other hand to alternately do the basic stroke on the cock and tickle and tease the balls. If you are doing this right, the skin will be taut around the balls and you will again have more access to the nerve endings.

Blow Jobs

As with touch, a cock generally gets sucked in one predictable way: someone puts it directly in their mouth and slides their lips up and down the shaft. A blow job is often approached as if it were exactly that: a job that needs to be done and gotten over with quickly. Check in with yourself and see what kinds of physiological and psychological arousal you can get out of giving a blow job, so that it feels good and fun for you. (See the section on touching for your own pleasure and incorporate those principles into giving a blow job.) You may like the sensation in your mouth or the feeling that you are powerful because you can give him so much pleasure and he is at your mercy. You may enjoy the feeling that you are being used. When men talk to us about blow jobs, what we hear most often is that blow jobs are much better if their partner is enjoying the experience.

Also, just as with oral sex on a woman, an interesting and exciting blow job starts out slowly and builds up. You can kiss from your partner's lips down his chest and across his thighs. Take your time before even getting to his cock to build anticipation, letting him know that he is about to get his cock licked and sucked, but not quite yet. Start by kissing his cock or lightly gliding your tongue across the shaft and head. Don't forget to kiss and lightly lick the balls as well. You might also take his cock and rub your face across it so that it touches your lips, your cheeks, even your forehead. Pay special licking attention to the frenulum, since it is one of the most sensitive parts of the cock on most men.

As you begin to lick the tip and tease it into your mouth, use your hands to continue tickling and teasing the balls. You can pull the skin on the shaft tight or circle the balls and pull them down, as you did when you were giving a hand job. Now you are just doing it in concert with your gentle licking, sucking, and teasing of the cock. As you move your head up and down his cock, your tongue is free to lick and flick across the shaft and frenulum. If his cock is large, use your hand as an extension of your mouth, again using spit to make sure that your hand or his whole cock is wet.

At some point, take a break from sucking his cock and put his balls in your mouth. Depending on their size, you may be able to fit only one or both of them in your mouth. Roll them around your mouth and suck them. Men, consider shaving your balls to make this a much more fun experience for your partner. As you are licking and sucking his balls, you can still use one hand to continue to stimulate his cock.

If you want, you can have him fuck your face: you hold still and he moves his cock in and out. You can also try deep throating. The easiest position to deep throat in is sixty-nine or modified sixty-nine, where you are not sitting on his face but kneeling at the side of his head. Make sure that your mouth isn't dry if you are going to try this. You will need lots of spit for lubrication. Tell your partner to hold still, then slowly open and relax the muscles in your throat and let his cock slide down. If you have a strong gag reflex, you may not get very far, but you can also allow yourself to gag just a little and see if that is a turn-on for you.

It is up to you whether you want to spit or swallow. As long as your partner does not have a sexually transmitted infection, semen is harmless, and you might actually end up with less of a bitter taste in your mouth if you just go ahead and swallow than if you hold it in your mouth and wait to spit it out. If you really don't like the idea of having cum in your mouth at all, ask your partner to let you know when he is about to cum so you can finish him off with your hand or let him finish himself off onto some part of your body (if that is a turn-on) or into a towel. You can also just use blow jobs as a warm-up to transition to some other sex act without his coming.

Intercourse

In our culture the term "sex" is interchangeable with "intercourse." We often don't count our other pleasurable experiences as sex unless intercourse happens. However, intercourse is not the be-all and end-all of sex. Some people love intercourse and others have no interest in it at all. It is important to talk openly about this in your relationship, accept each other's desires and boundaries, and see if you want intercourse to be part of your sex life. If you do enjoy intercourse, taking the time to warm up each other's entire bodies, including giving the woman some orgasms before going to intercourse, will ensure that you are both primed for a more pleasurable experience. If a woman's body is not warmed up, she is much less likely to orgasm during intercourse or to feel much of anything at all.

There are both men and women who do not come from intercourse. Some men may need to pull out and finish some other way, such as by receiving oral sex or masturbating, while some women may need to use their hands or a vibrator to help them come during intercourse. If you are a woman who is clit-oriented, sexual positions that allow you to rub your clit against your partner's pelvic bones (such as missionary position and woman on top) are more likely to lead to orgasms. Keeping the cock deep inside and doing circles, or moving the cock in and out a little bit, will be the most likely to sufficiently stimulate the clit. As a woman, you can use your hands to physically move your partner the way you want them to move when they are inside of you. Even if you need it slow and deep to be able to orgasm, you may also still really like it hard and fast. Tell your partner what you like best.

Some women can come during intercourse only by using their hand or a vibrator. If this is the case, try positions that allow room to get her hand or a vibrator involved. Modified missionary position, woman on top, and doggie style can be great positions to incorporate a vibrator of any size. If she is more G-spot-oriented, remember that the G-spot generally needs a lot of pressure; use positions that point the cock or dildo directly towards the G-spot. One of the best positions for G-spot stimulation is the modified missionary position, where the woman lies on her back and her partner kneels in front of her, with her butt on the top of his thighs. This way the cock or dildo points upwards toward the G-spot and gives it direct stimulation and plenty of pressure. The other great position is woman on top, where the woman is leaning back slightly so that she gets a lot of pressure on her G-spot. Doggie style can provide G-spot stimulation and is also a great position for women who come from their cervix, as it allows the cock or dildo to get as deep as possible. Make sure you experiment with different angles. If you find an angle that she really responds to, stick with it. Adding clitoral stimulation can create a great combination cervical-clit orgasm.

Most heterosexual encounters follow a predictable trajectory: kissing, touching, possibly oral sex, then intercourse that continues uninterrupted until the man orgasms. Both men and women think of male orgasm as the obvious end of every sexual experience. This implies that everything else that happens during sex is just a warm-up for the main event: the man's orgasm. For a much more varied and playful sex life, try switching it up. For example, oral or manual sex can be more exciting for some women after they have already been penetrated. Many women are capable of a few more orgasms once they have already come, and their partners can offer assistance. By breaking the expectation that sex ends with the man's orgasm, you can make your sex life much more varied and fun.

⌒

Journal opportunity: Men's Orgasms
Men: write about the your favorite way or ways reach orgasm.

If your partner is a man: write about the way you think your partner most likes to reach.

Anal Pleasure: The Final Frontier

There's a joke among sex therapists: Question: "How many times do women usually have anal sex?" Answer: "Once." Yep, that's the whole joke, but every sex therapist gets the joke because anal sex done badly is painful, and most anal sex is not done well. Many men also avoid anal pleasure because of homophobia. Anal play of all kinds can be extremely pleasurable for women and men, but most people have so many taboos, fears, or bad experiences that they don't even try it.

One wonderful outcome of anal play is enhanced intimacy, because you are sharing a very vulnerable part of yourself. It can also add a sense of naughtiness, because the asshole is thought of as a naughty, taboo part of the body. For both men and women, anal touch, oral-anal stimulation (sometimes called "rimming"), or light or full anal penetration (with a finger or toy) can be a way to more deeply arouse and engage the cock or clit, and anal play can help men and women cross over the edge to orgasm. Using a finger on or around the ass during oral sex is one way to play with anal stimulation. You can also use your fingers or a butt plug during manual stimulation or intercourse.

Before doing any anal play, it can be helpful to have a conversation about it. You can talk about your desires, your fears, and any boundaries you currently have around anal touch. Before engaging in any kind of anal play, make sure you have thoroughly cleaned your asshole. Some people prefer to do an enema before anal play, while others find that that makes it more messy. You may want to try it and see if it works for you. Cleanliness is especially important if you are going to be doing any oral-anal play, so that your partner doesn't ingest harmful bacteria. With anal penetration, usually there will not be any poop at first, but there may be some as you go deeper. It is important that you are okay with this if you want to play with anal penetration.

For most people the asshole needs to be approached slowly and gently, with lots of warm-up, if there is going to be any penetration. It is helpful to learn some anal massage techniques to gently relax and open the asshole up. In men the asshole is the only way to access and massage the prostate, which can often create more intense, explosive orgasms. You can also access a woman's G-spot through the asshole by inserting your fingers and doing the same "come hither" motion you would do in the vagina.

The first rule of anal play is to use large quantities of lube. The anus is not self-lubricating, so purchase lube—spit or vaginal lubrication is not enough to create a delightful anal experience. Also, if it goes in the ass, it doesn't go in the pussy. Make sure you use a different finger if you are going to stimulate your partner's ass and pussy in the same sexual encounter. If you want to have vaginal intercourse following anal intercourse, either use a condom for anal or wash very well in between; if you don't, she might get a bacterial infection. Finally, anal play isn't just about penetration by the penis. You can also use fingers, tongues, and toys for a deeply satisfying experience.

Bring All Your Sexy Tools Together

In this section we offered you an expanded menu of choices for your sexual pleasure. You learned about the social messages, harmful myths, and sexual challenges that hold you back from your full sexual potential as individuals and as a couple. You learned about your Hottest Sexual Movies and how to bring the touch, energy, story, and words of romance, passion, and dominance to a lover, as well as how to be a good submissive. You also explored other sexual movies and learned how to give and receive exquisite touch and share feedback.

All that you have learned in this book will help you Make Love Real, both emotionally and sexually. We hope that the tools and insights you have gained will help you have lasting, satisfying, passionate, and connected relationships and a lifetime of fun and fulfillment.

Feeling abandoned
- by family as a child and now
  never felt I belonged with them
  or part of the family, still don't

- Friends
  Lost contact with most friends as
  I stopped initiating contact.

Control
- Don't feel I have any control
in relationship with sonny
       most things done on his terms
but I do this to keep the peace
       Loose myself when I do this
  - or ~~have~~ can show my feeling and
desires

Fear
  - that if I do ~~show~~ my feelings or
exert my needs he will leave
  - ~~to show any~~ rejection
  - that I'm not enough

I feel sonny gets what he needs from
the relationship for what he is willing
to put in.
I don't feel my needs are considered by him,
which is playing on my insecurities

Printed in Great Britain
by Amazon